Forever Home

Forever Home

How We Turned Our House into a
Haven for Abandoned, Abused, and
Misunderstood Dogs—and Each Other

Ron Danta and Danny Robertshaw
and Larry Lindner

HarperOne
An Imprint of HarperCollins*Publishers*

FIRST EDITION

Designed by Kyle O'Brien

All photographs courtesy of Ron Danta and Danny Robertshaw, with the following exceptions, which are used by permission: p. 59: Karen Odom; p. 76: Jennifer Mackey, JCM Photography; p. 111: Dean Schink; p. 126: Clay Westervelt for Docutainment Films (docutainmentfilms .com); p. 141: Michael Schofield; p. 177 (top right and bottom): Michael Schofield; p. 192 (left): Jeff Gilbert; p. 210: Kim Tudor; p. 235 (top): Debbie Emerick for Meals on Wheels of the Palm Beaches (MOWPB .org); p. 235 (bottom): Judith K. Eisinger; p. 236 (top): Carissa Agnello; p. 236 (bottom): Elana Morgan; p. 247 (top): Michael Schofield; p. 247 (bottom): Larry Lindner; p. 250: Michael Schofield

Library of Congress Cataloging-in-Publication Data has been applied for.

ISBN 978-0-06-311287-2

22 23 24 25 26 LSC 10 9 8 7 6 5 4 3 2 1

In memory of our mothers, Norma Robertshaw and Eileen Danta, who shaped our love for animals and who no doubt are right now soothing bewildered dogs newly arrived to their realm.

Also, in memory of Danny's sisters, Kitts McQueen, Cheryl Roberts, and Lynne Nelson, and to Ron's sister, Diane Danta of Frankfort, Illinois. All of them have been kind to countless pups, including their younger brothers, whom they always accepted unconditionally.

Finally, to the millions of people around the globe involved in dog rescue—those working at shelters and related organizations as well as every single person who has ever adopted a dog that otherwise would have remained homeless. When you take in a dog, you are giving it not only love but also a voice. You are saying, "I hear you. You are safe now. You are not alone."

Contents

Prologue 1

1 Lost . . . 3

2 . . . and Found 18

3 Water Rising 39

4 Unanticipated Houseguests 60

5 Heart Breaking 77

6 Making It Official, Part 1 96

7 Blanket Hour 112

8 We Will Survive 127

9 Making It Official, Part 2 149

10 Smoke 165

11 On the Road 178

12 A Turn of Events 193

13 Broadening Our Horizons 218

14 Lifetime Promise 238

Epilogue 248

Acknowledgments 253

Prologue

The first sounds of toenails hitting the floor make their way to us through a light sleep. It's usually Lhasa apso mix Speckles who jumps down first. It took him forever just to get *on* the bed. Six months had to go by before he would even come into the bedroom at night. When we'd try to coax him to the mattress, he'd run out the door. During the day, when he wasn't darting away from us, he was snarling. Then the better part of a year passed before he made his way to the pillows, where he now wraps himself around Ron's head for his nightly repose.

We don't open our eyes but can sense the first weak rays of dawn straining to make their way through the shades. Wiggling follows, and we can feel some of the dogs begin to emerge from under the covers. We try to pretend that we can get a little more shut-eye before the day begins in earnest.

Isabelle, a liver-colored terrier with an adorable underbite, and Sweet Pea, a white Chihuahua-looking thing, are still perched at the very edge of the bed, as far from our feet as possible. It's going to take a while more for them. Beanie—she spends the night poking her head into the room, thinking through the risks as someone might before deciding whether to get on an intriguing but scary amusement park ride, until she finally loses her nerve and steals away. That's okay. Here, time's on her side.

It's too late to be able to tell the dogs to go back to sleep. They're more than stirring now and need to get outside before being fed. Still, we make an effort to fool ourselves into thinking we can doze just a few moments more.

And then Danny feels a weight on his chest. He opens his eyes to find himself looking directly at Busy Bee standing on top of him—all seventeen pounds of her, with all four of her legs. She's staring right back, with one blue eye and one brown one.

Before this, the poodle/miniature Australian shepherd mix, a puppy mill discard, has never even so much as come *near* the bedroom. Having lived in a cage her entire life until we took her in, never knowing either kindness or love, she is deathly afraid of people, and other dogs. She spends most of her time cowering in a corner of the kitchen.

But something has shifted for her. After months and months of keeping to herself and shaking when we tried just to lightly stroke her muzzle, she has courageously—boldly—decided to take a closer look, to consider that a better life awaits.

We look at each other and smile. It is going to be a good day.

Chapter 1

Lost . . .

Men at some time are masters of their fates.
—Shakespeare

But not always.
—Danny and Ron

Camden, South Carolina, 1979

DANNY

Moonpie ran right past the live oak saplings lining both sides of the long driveway the moment I set her down. Short and stout to the point that she was shaped like a tiny coffee table, she normally didn't have it in her to move so quickly. But watching her scamper with joy around the fields leading to the house, I could see that the little Jack Russell terrier—chestnut-colored with splotches of white—knew instinctively she had arrived at her new home and loved the freedom the farm was going to afford her. Johnny Cake, also a Jack Russell but far more slender, scrambled to catch up once I lifted him out of the pickup too, the pair of them romping and rolling and the white markings against Johnny's deeper-colored chocolatey brown fur clear even from a distance.

I brought up the rear with Number 7, my donkey that I named after the burro in the *Grizzly Adams* TV show. Wild Thing, a pony I rescued after he was found tied to the bumper of a rusted car in a trailer park, would join us a little later.

I was only twenty-five but had been doing well riding and training horses in hunter/jumper competitions and thought it was time to invest in a place of my own rather than continue renting. It was a heady feeling seeing my name on the deed: Daniel James Robertshaw.

The parcel, twenty-two acres, was situated on the outskirts of Camden. I named it Beaver River Farm, after the name of my mother's family farm in Rhode Island. I lived up north until I was three, before my parents came to North Carolina for my father's job as a manager at a textile plant.

The saplings—seven scraggly Charlie Brown Christmas trees on either side of the drive—were barely five feet tall. I could easily see over them as I approached the clearing with the farmhouse. It was a white bungalow with a wraparound porch built almost sixty years earlier, in 1920—too young to be an antique but definitely old enough to invoke the word "ramshackle."

The place was pretty much a mess. You could see even before you came right upon the house that it was badly weather-beaten. The two-horse barn out back was rickety, too, and the land was going to need tending. Scrub brush and old cars and barbed wire littered the fields. Cacti grew in the depleted soil, and broken-down fencing everywhere meant not a single field or paddock was truly suitable for animals.

That was okay. I knew I could tend to things gradually. My idea was to make it a place to kick back and provide a haven for animals requiring help—dogs, old horses, anything that needed saving. It wasn't a mission. It wasn't even really a plan. It was just the way I lived, the way I felt. If an animal was starving, I would be able to take it in and fatten it up. If I saw a dog on the road I wanted to be able to take care of it. I was going to be able to carve out my niche just as I wanted it.

While Danny settled in, only about an hour away . . .

RON

I was living in a trailer park with my wife, Paige, and our three dogs, crammed in and making ends meet. I worked forty hours a week at a 7-Eleven and another forty taking inventory at supermarkets and pharmacies. I had turned twenty-five earlier that year and had just moved to South Carolina to try to make a go of it in the show horse world. My work was in training horses and riders for hunter/jumper competitions, the spectacles where people on horseback sail gracefully over fences and other obstacles.

I had been training in my native Illinois, near Chicago, at a farm my parents had bought me, and was doing reasonably well. But the previous winter, the roof of the barn caved in as the result of a blizzard during which three and a half feet of snow had fallen in the space of twenty-four hours. I was teaching a lesson in the indoor arena when I started to hear a crackling sound. I looked up and saw the giant trusses near the ceiling kind of bowing down. I ran and opened the big door and told the two people to whom I was giving a lesson to run. Then I hurried and got the horses out, but almost immediately the entire indoors started going down in a domino effect and continued over to the stalls, where I was boarding thirty-five horses.

I managed to move them to another stable, but it, too, collapsed. Then I arranged for them to stay in a third stable, but the barn there had caved in by the time the horses arrived. Barns were falling apart all around because of the snow's weight, and I had to put the horses in my own outdoor ring until I finally was able to move them to a barn that was quite far away and where the snow wasn't falling as hard.

We rebuilt the barn and the indoor arena, but I had had enough of the cold Chicago weather and decided to head south. I had a friend who told me what a beautiful state South Carolina is.

My parents didn't approve of the relocation. When I was preparing to leave, they shut me down: "Ron, if you go, we will disown you." They had never spoken to me in such stark, resolute terms. It was a very difficult, emotional discussion, and finding out that I was going to have to choose between my parents and moving didn't come until right at the end. But I felt it was the right decision. And everything had already been set in motion.

I understood my parents' distress. They had spent much of their life savings to set me up in the horse business, even taking out a second mortgage for the farm. It didn't just have a barn and an indoor ring but also a club room and wonderful turnout pastures. The farm wasn't all of it, however. They had never approved of Paige—herself a horse rider—and the move hammered in the final nail. It was really my mother who felt so strongly about it, but my father went along. They went ahead and cut all ties, refusing to talk to me.

I was devastated, completely sucker punched. I had always been incredibly close to my parents. I hoped maybe things would right themselves, that they were just saying they would no longer talk to me because they were hurt and angry about my leaving.

Either way, my hands were too full to deal with it just then. Before Paige and I moved to South Carolina, we bought a five-acre parcel of land there to build a barn and some paddocks along with a small house so we could set ourselves up in business. But from the moment we arrived, nothing had gone right.

Ahead of making the trip down, we found an apartment that would allow pets, but when it came time to sign the lease upon arrival, the landlord said we could not have our dogs there and wanted us to give them up. That was not going to happen.

I grew up loving dogs. My parents would go down to the shelter every couple of months specifically to pick out old, sick dogs that no one was going to adopt and bring them home to enjoy a safe, loving hospice before they finally were done living.

At first Paige and I holed up with them in a motel room, the U-Haul in the parking lot with all our furniture and things. We had our Jack Russell, Sunny, along with gentle giant Tara—she was a Doberman—and Sammy the cocker spaniel. But that wasn't going to work for long. It wasn't just about being cramped. We couldn't afford the nightly bill.

But we couldn't afford a house, either. With the money we had spent on the land, we didn't have much left in savings, and it was dwindling fast because no one, we learned pretty quickly, was going to allow us to rent an apartment with three dogs. I finally bought a small mobile home as a stopgap solution—a poor one, because the dogs were not even allowed to roam around the trailer park. Everyone kind of gets just their own little patch. I would have to drive them to areas far from the park, where they could have good walks.

In the meantime, I was bleeding more money on the land we had purchased. It all needed to be cleared, and in every spot that the builders conducted a soil perc test to see where they could build a septic system and put a foundation for a barn and a house, water literally sprouted up in geysers. They were hitting springs, and the water table was too high to do anything. They would add fill to the land in spots to see if that would work, but drainage remained poor. The acreage was going to be unusable. We had spent $20,000 on the parcel and another $40,000 trying to make it suitable, all of it sunk money, in addition to the mobile home that I never had any intention of buying.

Finally, I caught a break. Scouting about for opportunities in the equestrian world, I met a woman who hired me to train horses on her property, where she had a little cottage that she let Paige and me live in. She briefly introduced us to Danny at a horse show in 1980.

Recalls Danny, "It was literally a 'So-and-So, meet So-and-So' kind of thing. They seemed like a nice young couple. I had no idea what they had been going through."

Nobody did, and trying to dig out from all the money that had been lost was only part of it. Paige had a serious addiction to pain pills, including Vicodin. She would mix the drugs with alcohol, making the problem particularly difficult. One time, I underwent extensive back surgery and was sent home with some of the most potent narcotics available to dull the pain. But they were giving me zero relief. I was in agony, having gone a week without any real sleep. I called the doctor to let him know the drugs he had prescribed weren't helping. He was baffled because his intention had been to keep me as comfortable as possible while I recuperated, but he felt he couldn't up the dosages any further without endangering my health.

Then, one night in bed I dropped one of the gelatin capsules as I was going to put it in my mouth, and when I squeezed it to pick it up from the mattress, the capsule opened, and I could see it was empty. Paige had been removing the medicine for herself and putting the capsules back together so I wouldn't notice.

I couldn't tell the doctor what happened; I always tried to protect Paige from her problem leaking out. Especially back then, there was tremendous stigma attached to drug and alcohol problems. I wanted to help her advance her riding career, too, as well as put the best face possible on my marriage. But I did confront her privately.

"How could you let me sit there and suffer?" I asked her, both hurt and angry. At first she denied it but then came clean and apologized and promised she'd never do it again. I didn't know at that point that until someone really owns their addiction, their word can never be trusted. But still, she had made that promise to me enough times in the past that when I had my prescription refilled, I knew to hide the medicine. Because I'm six foot eight, I could find spots that would be hard for her to reach, let alone discover—although sometimes she did, anyway.

Once I recovered from the back surgery, it was back to training horses. Danny and I would meet several more times on the show horse circuit throughout the early '80s, but only to say hello, or perhaps nod to each other if we happened to be eating at the same restaurant with clients.

DANNY

I was beginning to experience difficulties of my own, even though things had started out on such a promising note at the farm. The eldest of my three older sisters, Kitts—the family called her Kitsy—was struggling with a serious cancer of the gastrointestinal tract. At thirty-seven with a teenage son, she was still hanging on, but the prognosis was not encouraging. She was often in the hospital for treatment.

It was a constant worry. But that wasn't what drove me to make a visit home to North Carolina one late afternoon in 1983. I had just finished a horse show, and out of nowhere I felt a need to drive three hours out of the way and go to see my parents. I can't explain the urge that pulled me there, but there was no ignoring it, even though for most of my life I had had a fraught relationship with my father. He would call me a big sissy for missing a football when I was a boy. He probably didn't realize how painful those ribbings were—maybe he just meant to goad me on. But they stung.

It was probably difficult for him because he had been captain of the football team in college and I was his only son, having come to him unexpectedly when he was already forty. My parents had had my three sisters in short order, and I arrived on the scene much later.

"Jake got his son," people said. "The miracle finally happened." But I wasn't the miracle he had been dreaming of, not at all living up to his idea of what a son should be. I was sensitive about everything. If my parents fought, I thought it was because of me. I thought my mom started drinking because I didn't turn out the way my father wanted, and that made them not get along. I would get depressed, with headaches. I tried to hide it. I didn't want it to be just one more of "Danny's weaknesses."

It was never a question of whether my father loved me. I just don't think he knew what to do with me.

To his credit, he gave in to my mother and bought me my first horse—a pony for Christmas the year I turned ten. He never minded that I liked to ride. But he always wanted me to outgrow my obsession with it. He was concerned that I wouldn't be able to make a living at it, that I would reach my fifties and not be able to ride anymore. But for me, ever since I was young, being able to jump on a horse and go riding had been like having a tree house that I could escape to all by myself.

Dad and I made a cautious, unspoken truce—throughout my childhood and even as a young adult I never knew how to talk to him—and life went on.

He was very surprised when I walked through the door that day but also uncharacteristically thrilled to see me—not just glad, but truly happy. In retrospect, his reaction made sense in light of a recent scare. I had been in a serious twenty-seven-car pileup only a month earlier. People died. A fire on the side of the highway created thick black smoke that made it impossible for drivers to see. And although I was fine other than for some burns I had on my arms, the accident made it to the national news, and I was the last person involved who was accounted for. One highway patrolman

11

had burned to death. Even Moonpie suffered a burn that put a hole in her back when a truck next to our vehicle exploded, running off from me and not being found till the next day. I think that although my parents knew I was okay, they were still relieved to see me in person. The accident had left them shaken.

The house usually felt tense—Dad was often in a worried mood, particularly with my sister sick, and my mother would react by trying to paint a rosier picture but also by drinking. But everything had a light mood that afternoon that usually was missing. In fact, it was tax time, and Dad was always after me to try to be better about my books, but that day he laughed it off. Both Mom and Dad were in good spirits, and we stayed up late into the night talking and joking and swapping old family stories. We had never had an evening like that in our entire lives.

Sometime around 2 a.m. my father validated me in a way that will stay with me forever. "You know," he said, "I think you're going to make it in this horse world, and I think you're going to do well." It was the kind of thing children wait their whole lives to hear from their parents.

We finally all went to bed, and the next morning when I came into the kitchen, my mother was cooking a nice big breakfast for us that, as usual, included johnnycakes (which is how Johnny Cake was named). "Mom, where's Dad?" I asked. Whenever she made breakfast, he was always there reading the newspaper.

"He said he had a headache," Mom answered. "He went back to bed."

I went into his bedroom and saw that he was pretty blue, with very shallow breathing. I started CPR right away and asked my mother to dial 911 and to call my sisters because I felt sure he was going to the hospital. Kitts was already there for one of her cancer treatments. But by the time the paramedics arrived, he had already died right in my arms. He was sixty-eight. Kitsy was allowed out of the hospital for the funeral, tethered to an IV line. The day of Dad's death they had told her there was nothing else they could do for her and that it was just a matter of time.

RON

Around the time of Danny's father's passing, my fortunes began to turn for the better. I started gaining some notice as a trainer and had built back my finances to the point that Paige and I could afford to purchase a place of our own. Coincidentally just four and a half miles from Danny's farm, past cornfields and woods and beautiful, winding backroads characteristic of inland South Carolina, it already had a brick house with a gambrel roof in decent shape and pastures for horse turnout.

It was around then that the two of us started doing business together. As my own business grew, I needed a professional rider, so I started asking Danny to ride my clients' horses. Because we would cross paths occasionally at horse shows, I saw how good he was, along with learning what a good reputation he had as a horseman. He helped train Paige, too.

But while business was increasing, our personal lives continued to present difficulties. For one thing, my parents still refused to talk to me. I tried to reach out and call and send cards and gifts, and everything was returned unopened. Holidays like Christmas were very, very painful, leaving me with such an empty, lonely feeling. I hadn't even been able to tell them about anything that I had been going through. I was extremely close with my sister and grateful for that, but I still felt like my heart was ripping apart.

At the same time, Paige's addiction problem was tearing into the fabric of our marriage even more. She would kick and scream and bite if I hid her pain pills—even if she had asked me to in a bid to try to stop. She would swear at me. She finally agreed to go for treatment—twice. I had to take out a $250,000 loan because treatment away was so expensive. I was very private about it. I would tell people Paige had gone home to see her parents. I still wanted to protect her.

DANNY

I didn't know, even though I was Paige's riding trainer. I could see there were problems in their marriage. While the three of us were business colleagues rather than friends, it was a cordial relationship, and I could glean that something wasn't right; there was a kind of tension. However, I still had no idea what she was going through—or what Ron was going through, struggling with the situation.

I was also too preoccupied to try to put much of a lens on it. During Paige's first time away, Kitts finally succumbed to the cancer ravaging her body. She was forty. It felt like another hole was left in my family. Both she and my father were gone too soon.

RON

I didn't know Danny well enough to go to the funeral, but just around the time of Kitts's death, the treatment center called me while Paige was still there and said, "We want to enroll you in Al-Anon. It's a program for family members."

I was, like, "Why do I need to enroll in something? I don't drink. I'm not doing drugs."

They explained that alcoholism is a family disease; it affects everyone in the household. I balked at the recommendation.

Then a third member of Danny's family died—his mother.

DANNY

I was in New York City for a horse show at Madison Square Garden. I had just gotten to my hotel room when I saw the red light flashing on the phone and burst into tears. I knew before I even listened to the message. She had broken her hip a while back and kept complaining about pain, even though Mom was not a complainer. The doctor kept pooh-poohing her, but a workup by a second doctor showed that what seemed like residual hip pain was actually bone cancer.

She spent the last few months of her life bedridden. Johnny Cake, who I gave to her as a puppy before he came to stay with me at the farm, would not leave her side. I was told she was not allowed to have pets in her room because they would make it unclean with their hair and dander and tracking in dirt from outside, but every time I opened the door, he would run in and jump up next to her. When I tried to grab him, he'd scoot under the bed. I'd get down on my knees to take him, at which point he'd run to the other side, and I'd go around to try to get him from that end. Finally, I realized, my mother was dying. She wanted his company, and what was she going to gain by my forcing him to stay out of the room? He was with her as she took her last breaths.

It was November 1989. In the space of six years I had lost both of my parents and one of my sisters, all while I was in my twenties and thirties. My mother's death might have been the worst blow of all. While my father was perennially frustrated with me until that wonderful reconciliation at the very end, my mother always accepted me for who I was. It was in fact she who instilled in me my love for animals.

Very often, when I was young, she would tell me stories at bedtime about growing up with all kinds of animals on the farm, and I was enthralled by her reminiscences. There was a dog, Snyder Ash Barrel, who was her constant companion when she was a girl, never leaving her side. There was a white cat, Snowball, and her four kittens that my grandmother discovered in one of her kitchen drawers; a little pony called Leafy who pulled a cart. I looked forward to hearing these stories because they calmed my heart, and it was just so easy to fall asleep after that.

My mother also taught me about animals who had been abandoned and were at risk of being put to sleep. She'd take me down to the local shelter now and then to choose a dog with particularly sad eyes. We'd bring it home and nurse it back to happiness.

RON

Paige and I knew Danny well enough by the time of his mother's death that we attended her funeral out of state. It was the day she was laid to rest that I realized I had to make a decision.

The live oak saplings—seven scraggly Charlie Brown Christmas trees on either side of the drive—were barely five feet tall and no higher than the fence when Danny first bought the farm. It was easy to see beyond them to the house.

Danny, age 6, with a dog that he and his mother brought home from the local shelter.

Ron as a little boy with his first dog, Sandy, and his sister, Diane.

Chapter 2

. . . and Found

We are still captains of our souls.
—Winston Churchill

Agreed.
—Danny and Ron

RON

Paige and I were at the same horse show in New York as Danny when he learned his mother had died. We stayed in the same hotel, in fact. Things were not going well for us, to say the least. Paige invited a man to the show whom she had met while going for treatment, and he came to Madison Square Garden to watch her compete.

I was extremely embarrassed. She was letting our entire world know that even though we were married she was interested in someone else. I didn't want to make matters any worse while we still had horses to show, so we didn't get into any heated discussions in New York. But as we drove down from Manhattan to North Carolina for the funeral, we had it out. She confirmed my suspicions and said that yes, she had been seeing the guy.

It felt like more than a major slap in the face. I had given up a lot financially to support her and was also supportive through years of her addiction, and I felt betrayed—more so because she let it all out there for everyone to see when I'd worked so hard to keep her drug and alcohol problems a secret in order to protect her.

It all kind of crystallized from there. Not that I hadn't been working things over in my mind. While I'd dismissed the idea of going to Al-Anon a few years earlier, I did finally relent—and learned a lot in the process that helped me cope with this moment. It was one of the best things I could have done for myself.

Al-Anon taught me first of all that we are responsible only for ourselves. In other words, I was not going to be able to fix Paige. Only Paige could fix Paige. This was particularly difficult for me because I see myself as someone who takes charge and solves problems. I don't just sit around. But I came to realize that no matter what I did—if I bought her a new horse—I couldn't make her happy, because she had to had to *want* to find herself in life. She had to want to become sober. It wasn't I who could make that happen.

It was hard to come to terms with because one of the things that drew me to Paige in the first place was that she was susceptible. Rescuing her was a role in which I felt comfortable. Also, she was a little bit on the wild side, and I was raised in a very conservative household, so I found her free-spiritedness kind of enticing even though it turned out to be destructive. And once my parents totally cut me off, the last thing I wanted to do was have no marriage, to be completely by myself.

But here's the key piece. By going to Al-Anon I learned that even though she was on the downward spiral of a wild ride, it was okay to rescue *myself*, to learn about myself, and to *be* by myself. That tool gave me the key to freedom—to realize that I did not have to continue on this path. Her route, with or without the man in her life, didn't need to be my route, too. I didn't just have to accept the things that were happening.

It took time—years, really. It's not like it all happened in the space of a meeting or two. But you could say her affair was the straw that broke the camel's back. Part of what made it have to come to something that drastic was that it was not so easy back then—even though it was already the late 1980s, not really all that long ago—to come out as gay. I had feelings inside. I found Danny very handsome. But you fight yourself. You wonder, is this how everybody else feels at times? And Paige was very, very attractive. She modeled for Ralph Lauren. I liked having her on my arm.

And if I was being really honest with myself, I knew that I was using her in that way. She was my shield against anybody thinking I might be gay—my shield against my shame about not having enough self-worth to admit to myself who I was—and I was willing to put up with a lot because of that.

In the end, our staying together wasn't serving either of us. We both calmed down by the time we reached Wilmington, and the day of Danny's mother's funeral we had lunch, where I felt freed up to the point that I could put closure to my marriage. It was mutual, really, the decision to divorce. But the determination from my end to dissolve our union did finally give me the permission to look after my own needs. I realized I didn't need to deny myself.

The thing was, at that point, even though I now admitted to myself that I had feelings for Danny, I wasn't really sure of what I was looking for. I had yet to find myself in life. I had spent most of my twenties and half of my thirties as Paige's boyfriend and husband, her caretaker. So I had to figure out who *I* was, *what* I was, and what I wanted.

Remarks Danny, "This wasn't like, 'Woo-hoo, I'm out of this now!' It was very hard on Ron. He took his marriage vows very seriously, and his commitment to Paige was what severed his relationship with his parents. They did not like that Ron left Illinois, but they disliked his wife even more. He had put his neck on the line over something that cost him what had been his most enduring emotional attachments."

DANNY & RON

It was in the wake of the divorce from Paige and the death of Danny's mother that the two of us started to *really* talk and express our feelings. There's nothing like mutual vulnerability to make for perfect timing.

Before the split, we had never been alone in the same room together, even when we started doing business as a kind of tag team, Ron teaching riders and Danny helping horses get the hang of hunter/jumper activities by riding them. But now we began to socialize by ourselves, to go out to dinner. "I started opening up to Danny," Ron says, "going through a rough time as I was after the breakup. Danny was there for me."

"I felt the same way," Danny says. "He was easy to talk to, and I felt for him."

We discovered there was much we had in common, including how we felt about animals, particularly abandoned or abused ones. It turned out both of our first dogs had been hit by cars and died on impact when we were kids, and we learned we both had mothers who had instilled in us a love for animals in need. Then, too, as boys, we'd each rather run over to a neighbor's barn and play with the horses—or save turtles and birds—than throw around a ball with the other boys in our neighborhoods.

We learned as well that we both had a habit of going down to the local shelter every month or so and picking up a couple of dogs that were on the list to be euthanized, bringing them home, and getting friends to adopt them—or just holding on to them until someone would take them. Or we'd pick up an abandoned dog at the side of the road.

"I don't know that our feeling for animals was the clincher for our relationship," Danny comments, "but it strengthened what was beginning to feel like a very mutual bond. So many animals haven't done anything to anybody. Their only infraction is that they were born and were now considered disposable, and neither of us could bear that."

Along with finding out that we had similar interests, we could see there was a ying and yang to the way we expressed our emotions. "Because I had been through so much loss when I was still relatively young," Danny says, "I was already schooled in the truth that things happen constantly, that you can expect that something bad is going to occur and just need to try to figure out how to deal with it when it does. So even though I might be very upset internally when tragedy strikes, I don't go to pieces, because

I've already been waiting for it. I just try to figure out how I'm going to handle this next thing.

"But while I'm not that readable, Ron is an instant reactor. He's definitely the take-charge type of the two of us, the one who makes plans and sees them through, and his assuming the lead on the business of life is fine with me. But he emotes more openly. For instance, at the end of his marriage, you could easily see how crushed he was. I suppose his ability to unleash his feelings like that also helped me to let go in front of *him* sometimes. And that was freeing, of course, and brought us closer, allowing us to explore deeper feelings for each other."

Still, for all our commonality and the way our temperaments complemented each other, Danny held off. "When Ron realized he was gay, I didn't want it to become an 'us' thing at that point," he recalls.

"I liked him better than anyone else I had been with. But I still needed time to sort things through. I wasn't sure I was ready to jump into something new. I felt very used up, not only because of a couple of prior relationships that had failed but also because of all the deaths in my family.

"Also, Ron was a tall, handsome man, and I felt there were a lot of people he deserved to meet before getting together with someone in a serious way. I knew I was the go-to person for him at that point, but because he was newly gay, I thought that was only going to last a little while before other guys started showing interest and things went in a different direction.

"Yet in moments where I could put my hesitation aside, I knew that I liked being with Ron. He didn't try to mold me in any way, the way people will do sometimes. He has a very take-charge personality, and he's much more tightly wound than I am.

I'm far more easygoing. The thing was, he was fine with that. He wanted me to be the person I was, not some version of me, and I found that very appealing."

In the end, the plan to hold off didn't work very well.

To console Danny after his mother died, Ron surprised him with a little strawberry blond Norfolk terrier named Chloe. "We were just beginning to be a couple," Ron says. "But I wanted Danny to have this gift, something to make him happy in the wake of his mother's passing. I guess you could also say it was a gesture of courtship. Chloe was related to a Norfolk terrier that I once had. By putting her in Danny's arms, I was connecting us to each other a little more, re-creating us as a family. I knew that a dog was an audacious gift to give someone early in a relationship, but I felt ready to take the chance."

"He read me right," Danny says. "From the day I first touched Chloe, from that very moment, she was as much a part of me as any dog in my life. She was my heart. I can name other dogs that I have loved, but I don't know—we just had some kind of see-through-each-other bond. It didn't develop. It didn't grow. It was just always there."

Of course, Chloe was also a connection to Danny's mother, which gave her even more special meaning. Maybe that's why it wasn't very long after Chloe entered the scene that we did decide to move in together, Danny coming to live at Ron's house while we held on to Beaver River Farm to train horses, and Chloe helping to heal Danny's heart while he mourned his mother's loss. It was a kind of yours-mine-and-ours situation. Danny brought along Moonpie and Johnny Cake, who now roomed not only with Chloe but also with Ron's dog, Tara the Doberman. Paige had taken the cocker spaniel in the divorce, and Ron's own Jack

Russell, Sunny, had been stolen while he and Paige lived in the cottage in between inhabiting the mobile home and buying the house.

"I couldn't figure out at the time what might have happened," Ron says. "Sunny never would have just run off. Although money was still tight at that point, I put ads in the newspaper offering a $1,500 reward for his return. I was beside myself."

"Probably about three weeks after he was gone, a story broke on the local news about guys in trucks coming by people's properties and scooping up small dogs as bait to bring out aggression in larger dogs used in a dog-fighting ring. I couldn't bear to think about how Sunny had met his end. It was the first I had ever heard about dog fighting."

The abduction meant that after the divorce it was just Ron and Tara for a while, and whatever homeless dogs Ron took in on a temporary basis until he could find a home for them. But the house was now filled up again with dogs, and Tara and Danny's newly arrived pets got on famously. Tara would gentle herself in front of her smaller companions, getting down to their level with inviting play bows, while Johnny Cake in particular would lick her face. They'd all run around together playing chase in the side yard; life rolled forward, happily.

And before the two of us knew it, the first anniversary of Danny's mother's death was upon us. It would have been impossible to miss, as it coincided with the annual National Horse Show at Madison Square Garden in New York. We each went every year.

The prior year, while Danny entered his hotel room to find the phone's red light flashing with what was going to be heart-rending news, Ron and Paige had checked into another room. Now we would be staying together.

As we were packing the car to drive north to New York City, out of Danny's mouth popped the words "I need to bring Chloe with us." It was a strong pull.

Ron understood. Chloe would always sit on Danny's lap when the two of them watched TV. She could read Danny, too. "She wasn't a barker or a whiner," Danny says. "She was an eye follower. Wherever we were, my eyes would connect with hers, and she could divine the emotion of anything I was ever thinking about. She would know whether to come over all jiggly and happy or simply to approach me solemnly so I could just pick her up and hold her. She just sort of knew how to celebrate every emotion that I was experiencing; she was always on target for it."

She slept next to Danny, too. "She would stay right by my ribs, a little above my waist, where my elbow could wrap around her," Danny says. "She would position herself on the bed before I got there, and her little tail would wag when I entered the bedroom—'Now I know you're here.' Then she'd just look at me, and I would understand to pull the covers up over her head, and we'd get into position. I'm not a great sleeper. I toss and turn a lot. But she'd always adjust to whatever movements I made. That's how we started out every single night."

Still, Ron didn't think it would be good for Chloe to bring her to a hotel in a strange place and leave her stuck by herself in the room all day. "Danny," Ron answered, "we're going to be staying in the heart of New York City. We can't bring a dog to this hotel."

Despite misgivings, Danny finally acquiesced, and we finished packing the car and were on our way. And then: "I need to go back and get her."

We were already on the interstate by that point. "We can't take a dog to the city," Ron said. "It won't be dog-friendly."

In addition, we were first going to the Pennsylvania National Horse Show in Harrisburg and then to the Washington International Equine Show in DC. It would have been too much for little Chloe.

A couple of weeks later, after competing in Pennsylvania and Washington and finally wending our way into Manhattan through the Holland Tunnel, we checked into the same hotel as the year before—this time into the same room together. Preternaturally, perhaps, it happened to be the very room Danny had checked into when he learned his mother died. What were the odds? The hotel, right near Madison Square Garden, was huge.

Several days passed and we had a very successful show, with Danny winning the championship. When we arrived back at our hotel room that night flush with triumph and celebration, we could see immediately that the red phone light was flashing. It was 7:30 in the evening, just like the year before. Danny immediately started crying. "Chloe's dead," he said.

"You're being maudlin," Ron told him. "Everything's fine." Ron then responded to the blinking light. The young woman taking care of Chloe and the other dogs had left a message to call home immediately. He placed the call and burst into tears as soon as he started listening. Danny was right. Chloe was gone. A truck was delivering horse feed just when she had been let out, and the driver didn't see her and ran her over. She died on impact.

"After Chloe's death," Danny says, "it was the first time in my life that I felt I didn't need another dog. Before, when a dog died, I wanted to save another one in that dog's honor. But this time, I was absolutely 'No way.' It had been an emotional period in the wake of my mom dying, and even if I just went down to the barn, Chloe could stay inside my jacket when it was cold and cuddle there. If she were a person, we would have completed each other's sentences.

"I never wanted to let myself be close to another dog again after that loss. I would always help with *rescuing* dogs, I decided. Both Ron and I would each pick up a dog from a shelter or the side of the road here and there and find someone to give the animal a home. But I could not risk loving one."

Ron saw it differently. After giving Danny a couple of months to process the loss of Chloe, he brought home Ebenezer, a wire-haired miniature dachshund in what is called wild boar color; the tips of his hairs were dark, while more toward the base they were shaded kind of like wheat. Ebenezer had been raised in a puppy mill in Kentucky, spending his life in a dark basement.

"I stayed with him in the bathroom until Danny came home," Ron says. "When Danny saw him, he picked him up and started to cry. The little dog was exceedingly timid, very scared."

"I was furious despite my reaction," Danny says. "I knew what Ron was up to, and I wasn't having it. But Chloe must have sent him, because he stole my heart in much the way I was determined never to let it get stolen again.

"I *told* you not to do this," he recalls saying to Ron. "'I do not want another dog. I don't want it.' But I wouldn't let him go. He was such a sad-looking little creature, with those long, droopy ears and such a forlorn, worried look in his big brown eyes, as if to say, 'What's going to happen next?' It made him so irresistible. I just didn't want to go through the pain yet another time.

"Still, I knew that every angry thing I was saying to Ron I didn't mean, and I know he knew it, too. But I had to get those words out. I had to let something go. I didn't consciously know what I was doing, but as angry and conflicted as I felt, I knew the dog wasn't going back. He was here to stay. I could have told myself that I was going to make the choice to be cold and ignore him, but the choice had already been made. I was going to love living with him."

"Even though Danny was acting upset, I knew it was not really anger but pain," Ron says. "He was still grieving over Chloe, over his mother. I knew he needed to open up his heart and love another dog. But I also thought I should bring home one that looked really different from Chloe. Ebenezer started out very different in temperament, too—very introverted, very scared. In the beginning he would shake and cower and exhibit a pitiful withdrawn look. And, of course, with Danny letting down his guard the moment he laid eyes on him, he became the nurturing father to this little puppy, and they formed an incredible bond. It was Danny who named him, after his maternal grandfather. We used to call him Nezer."

"He became kind of like my pocket buddy," Danny says. "I think the shortness of Chloe's life made her shoes hard to fill, but he became special in his own way. Anytime you picked him up and held him, he would stick his little long nose up and give you a lick on the chin. And as he acclimated to his new life, he could be playing with other dogs in the yard, but if he'd see me he'd leave everybody and come running. I was his favorite dog."

"The cutest thing Nezer used to do," Ron says, "was, when he wanted attention, he would sit up on his butt like a gopher or groundhog and patiently stare until you noticed he was there and gave him some love. You could be talking on the phone, and all of a sudden he'd be sitting there like that just staring up at you."

Over time, Nezer's sadness left him. He never became a people dog. Other than the two of us, he wasn't interested in even acknowledging other people's presence. Some people probably thought he had no personality. But he came alive for us, always ready to interact and enjoy together time.

And he enjoyed the other animals we brought into the house. One of them was Buttercup, a papillon mix that had been turned in at our local shelter. "I happened to be standing in the front office," Ron says, "when this woman pulls into the parking lot in a Mercedes. She walks in holding Buttercup with both hands, as far away from her body as she could, rings and a Rolex watch draped over her. 'I don't want my dog anymore,' she declares, just like that, and signs the papers to turn her over. I told the shelter director right then and there that I would take Buttercup home with me.

"She was—and still is at twenty—the friendliest and calmest dog in the world—not nervous at all and supremely secure. Until she became very old, she would sit up in a begging position, kind of the way Nezer did, except you could say to her, 'Buttercup, wave!' And she would wave and wave at you like the queen in her carriage—but with more of a lightheartedness. She knew her antics were making us happy. When she was young and we took her places, she was always a big hit on the golf cart we ride to make our way around the acres and acres of rings and stables at horse shows. She would sit straight up and wave at passersby to be admired and cooed over. She and Nezer used to love to hang out together, nestled on the couch, on our bed, or chasing a ball in the yard."

Buttercup and Nezer also did fine when we took in new homeless dogs. The most we ever brought home at any one time was twenty-seven. The local shelter, a disease- and bacteria-ridden hellhole, was shutting down for a floor-to-ceiling sterilization. Whichever dogs were not adopted by a certain time on a certain day were going to be euthanized. We waited until just before the deadline, figuring we'd take the four or five dogs that would be left. But twenty-seven was the final count for those on Death Row, and although we had never had that many dogs with us before, we could not let them die for no good reason. So home they came with us, some staying in the house, some staying mostly outside, and some staying at Beaver River Farm with people we had hired to take care of the horses there. It was easy for us to see them every day when we came to train, but that was the only easy part. Little could we have figured what a steep learning curve would be built into taking care of so many new dogs at once.

Fortunately, none of them were aggressive toward each other, but as we soon found out, none of them were spayed or neutered, so there was some rivalry going on among certain male dogs with a few of the females coming into heat. We had to keep them separate from one another and also keep the impregnable females separate from *all* the males. It took putting some dogs in pens—portable kennels—creating fencing in spots, and keeping other dogs in their own horse stalls. It also took moving certain dogs around, from inside to out, from farm to house, and vice versa. "We just had to be creative," Danny says.

One dog, we came to realize, already *was* pregnant—and pretty far along. (A dog pregnancy lasts only nine weeks.) She had to have her own whelping space that absolutely none of the other dogs could get to. The last thing she needed was a dozen dogs poking around once she went into labor and her puppies were born. We also had a lot of questions about her that we needed to have answered. Could she have her shots while pregnant? (Not a great idea, we found out.) Could she be given a flea bath? (Yes, but it had to be a certain brand.)

There were other challenges, too—none of which we were ready for but had to tackle. One of them was spaying and neutering all the dogs, which, Ron relates, "was a major expense." We also had to clean all the dogs one way or another. Some had been wallowing in their own urine and feces. The stench was overpowering. Others needed flea and tick medication, and we also had to go through a process of determining whether any had kennel cough or other upper respiratory diseases. Certain types of those breathing illnesses can be very contagious, and we weren't going to let the visiting dogs mix with our own dogs until those questions were settled.

Then there was the wear and tear on the house. Some of the dogs urinated on the wood floors and oriental rugs throughout all the rooms; they chewed the leather furniture. "The couch and chairs were glove leather," Ron says. "Fifteen thousand dollars. To walk in and see a hole in the arm or a hole in the seat doesn't thrill you. And yet you can't turn on a dog for destructive behavior. No one made us take them in. They simply hadn't yet learned about or hadn't been exposed to living in a house. They didn't know anything about manners; no one had trained them."

"We installed baby gates," Danny comments, "trying to fence off little areas, and also kept a couple of dogs in the laundry room, but the house took a huge beating. They chewed on the legs of the cocktail table, the end tables, the edges of the wooden bed frame."

Still, for all that, and for all the anxiety we experienced by jumping in with both feet and *then* having to learn all the logistics, we were glad to have been able to save the dogs, bring them into better health, and eventually adopt them all out to other people in the horse world, including the new litter (of seven puppies). We knew they would have good lives as loved family members where they wouldn't have to vie for space and attention with dozens of others.

We took care of a lot of cats during those early years with each other, too. Before we were together as a couple, a gray tabby would regularly dart across Danny's farm. "I never touched her, not wanting to scare her," Danny says, "because she was feral. But one day she rubbed up against me. I took her to the vet to see if she was free from feline leukemia, upper respiratory problems, and all that, and she was. Then other cats started coming by."

When Ron came on the scene, we actually started trapping vulnerable cats—from dumpsters behind restaurants, bloodied at the side of the road from speeding cars, scavenging near trash cans. We'd take them to the vet to make sure they were okay, pay whatever bills were necessary to heal them, then turn them loose. But they hung out anyway. We needed to make sure they were safe from the dogs we were keeping at the farm, as well as from the horses. Cats can usually skedaddle very quickly, but as it was, that very first gray tabby that decided to become friends with Danny was chased and killed by one of the dogs. So we built the Kitty Hilton.

At the time, we were up to six horse stalls in the small barn behind the farmhouse, and instead of keeping hay in the lofts above them, we fenced them off with chicken wire so the cats could hang out. We even made a chicken-wire-enclosed "bridge" that crossed from one side of the barn to the other overhead, and from there the cats could walk to a spot with food and toys or sprint down a carpeted shoot that would take them outside to a large enclosed catio that we built. It had a tree in it and wooden, carpet-covered perches we constructed at different levels where the felines could sun themselves. Cats like to be high up; they evolved from tree dwellers.

They generally didn't like to be touched by us—most remained feral—but this way they could be kept safe. We fed them and changed their water every day and also once a week changed their litter. And they, in turn, helped us with a pigeon problem we were having, keeping the birds at bay and stopping them from bothering the horses after our own attempts had failed. People had recommended that we just kill the birds, but we were glad to have found a nonviolent means of convincing them to leave the property.

Others animals came to live at the farm, too—chickens, from whom we get our eggs to this day and whom we feed when we arrive to train horses each morning, rabbits, donkeys, sometimes a mule (a donkey crossed with a horse), even a fawn at one point. Cows came later—some of them dairy cows destined for slaughter because their milk production wasn't what it should have been.

Even a couple of mice made their way into our lives. Long before we were officially a dog rescue, the same woman would always come and look after the dogs we had taken in when we were on the road at horse shows. One winter she started complaining about two mice that ran across the kitchen counter every night— she was afraid of them. She told us she'd hired a pest control company to take care of them, and when we came home from one of the shows, Ron found some of those gooey, sticky traps in the laundry room. He threw them all out—"I did not want mice sticking to those things and slowly dying"—and drove over to

Walmart to buy some humane traps, the kind with the little door that shuts behind the mouse as it goes in to get the cheese.

"One night I was cooking dinner," Ron says, "and all of a sudden I hear a little *dink*. We had caught Mouse Number One. I called out to Danny—he was in the bedroom—and told him we had one of the mice and asked, 'Will you take it down to the barn'—there's a barn at the house as well as at the farm—'and turn it loose?' He comes into the kitchen while I'm cooking, and he looks at me and he says, 'Do you know it's going to be fourteen degrees tonight, and this mouse has been living in a heated house this winter? I'm not going to turn it out in fourteen-degree weather.'

"With that he pulls out a little cheese grater from one of the cabinets, goes over to the refrigerator, takes some cheese, grates a bit, and puts it in a small dish along with some horse grain and other food—a mouse buffet. Then he gets a small plastic cup and saws it off to make a little water dish, and then the next thing I see—I'm still cooking—is that he comes in with a cardboard box and starts putting nesting stuff in there. He's creating a home for this mouse, okay?

"Once he puts the mouse in its new home, we catch the second mouse in another humane trap, and I know not even to attempt to ask him to take it to the barn. The second mouse goes in the box, too.

"The next day the cold front was over and we were going to do the official turning loose of the mice. Well, Danny puts the mouse box in my Ford Excursion and drives down to the barn to let them out. Except one of the mice got out of the box, so he ended up turning only one loose. After waiting about three days, he confessed, 'I have something to tell you. Don't get alarmed, but one of those mice is living in your car.'"

Of course, that was nothing compared to the year Danny surprised Ron with baby ducklings for his birthday, hiding them in a kiddie splash pool in the laundry room until their quacking gave them away. Or the year he surprised Ron with a donkey of his own, who turned out to be quite a handful, beginning with his pooping all over our brand-new Tahoe on his way to his new home.

It was a happy time, and we loved getting to know each other better and better as we continued to save animals, mostly dogs, giving them the medical care they needed and subsequently getting equestrian friends of ours to adopt them and provide them with good homes.

Then Ebenezer suffered a setback; he had a seizure. Imaging at the doctor's office suggested a small brain bleed, and the vet put him on phenobarbital. He never seized again. But less than a year later, he required surgery for an intestinal blockage—he had swallowed part of a toy, as he was prone to do. He loved pulling the yellow fur off tennis balls.

The recovery was much tougher than the surgeon anticipated, with Nezer remaining lethargic and weak and finally needing a blood transfusion. He had to spend eight or nine days at the hospital. We finally were able to bring him home, and he seemed himself for three or four days, until the weakness returned. It was the week before Easter. We took him back to the clinic, where they conducted an ultrasound and discovered that he was leaking fluid into his abdominal cavity where they'd sewn his intestine after removing the blockage.

The suggestion was to open him up again, cut out the leaky part, and splice the two ends of his intestine back together once more. But when they went back in, they discovered tumors in the area. And doing research through the original medical records, they found that what was originally thought to be a tiny brain bleed was actually a brain tumor that had now metastasized to organs in his abdomen.

We waited a few more days, but Ebenezer wasn't able to rally. You could just see the look of surrender in his eyes. It was Easter Sunday. We looked at each other and knew it was time to let him cross the Rainbow Bridge that dogs are said to traverse as they pass to the other side.

The date was March 27, 2005. Little Nezer had been with us fourteen years. Of course other dogs had come into our lives and then left this world. But Nezer was the dog who had been with us, if not from the beginning, at least almost from *our* beginning. He was on the scene long before Buttercup, his ever-happier and more comfortable life with us running parallel to our own ever-deepening commitment to each other.

We stroked his muzzle and ears as the doctor injected the drug that would send him gently to sleep, crying without reserve, and later had his ashes put in a wooden box, which we have kept to this day. A vet once told us, "As much as you love someone, that's how much you will grieve."

But there wasn't going to be much time to mourn, or to reflect. Life was about to become very heady—and more dog-centric than we ever could have anticipated.

After Ron's divorce, it was just Ron and Tara the Doberman, along with Wassail the cat, picked up by the side of the road one day.

Danny, Johnny Cake, Number 7 the donkey (at left), and an Amazon parrot named Repito hanging out at the farm. Repito came home with Danny after flying onto his shoulder at a horse show.

Chapter 3

Water Rising

The car radio crackled as we fiddled with the dial. We were making the eight-hour drive home to South Carolina after working a horse show in Lexington, Kentucky, when the first predictions started coming through that Hurricane Katrina would hit New Orleans. Outside the air-conditioned Ford Excursion, when we would stop at the side of the road to let one of the dogs take a piddle, we could see the highway shimmering in the August heat. We were up to about five or six traveling dogs at this point.

We weren't terribly worried that we would get caught in the storm on the way back—the hurricane was going to be making landfall 750 miles to the south. But we wondered where it would turn after that. After hitting the Gulf, would it drift to the right toward Florida and then head up the coast through Georgia and the Carolinas? That could have a direct impact, as we were slated to spend only one night at home before driving nine hours south to Wellington, Florida.

We had recently bought a modest second home there. It hadn't been in the plans, but during a previous trip to Wellington, Danny was riding his bicycle one day trying to regain his fitness after his own back surgery and serendipitously came upon someone nailing a FOR SALE sign to a home with a large backyard. It was close to the horse farm where we worked, and we also knew there was plenty of land for turning out the dogs, so we went for it.

It made good economic sense. Year after year we needed to rent a house for four months or stay in a hotel that offered long-term arrangements, because Wellington has an annual Winter Equestrian Festival where we earn a sizable portion of our keep, training horses and riders. And rentals are expensive; the annual festival is the largest equestrian competition in the world, with hundreds of thousands of attendees from more than forty countries descending on the area. It's also always difficult to find a place that will let you bring your dogs.

Fixing up the house was a good distraction for Danny, as well. He was used to being very active with the horses and found rehabilitation from the surgery tedious, spending a lot of his time at dog shelters. "I was always frightened when I couldn't get him on the phone," Ron says, "because that meant he was at the Palm Beach County Animal Shelter. When I finally would be able to get hold of him, he'd say casually, 'Oh, by the way, I have a car full of dogs.' I was about to put a tracking collar on him so I could know if he was driving to go get some more dogs when we already had so many in our care."

The newly purchased Wellington bungalow was strictly for winter use, but we were going down at the end of the summer to do some work on the place—painting, ripping off old wallpaper, installing new blinds, things like that.

The weather reports on the car radio grew more ominous as we crossed from Kentucky into Tennessee. "This could be one of the largest, most catastrophic hurricanes in history," one meteorologist was saying. It put a pit in our stomachs—not just for the people but also for the animals. If the levees didn't hold up, more of New Orleans would flood. It wasn't just us, of course. The whole country was gripped by the impending disaster.

After a night at home in South Carolina—dropping off the trailer with the golf cart that we use to get around at horse shows, doing laundry, packing suitcases—we headed south on the nine-hour drive to Florida. We were not worried about the weather for ourselves at that point. We had stayed up very late watching the Weather Channel's projected path of the hurricane, and it showed the storm going nowhere near the east coast. At dawn we piled the dogs into the car while the storm predictions and warnings of water surges in New Orleans kept worsening.

Once we arrived at the house in Wellington, we kept the TV on day and night to hear and watch what was going on while we worked to get the new place in shape. Our hearts, along with the rest of the country's, were in knots. The looming orb of the storm as shown by radar filled the entire Gulf. Once the hurricane came ashore, levees did break, of course, and the scenes proved devastating. Never could we have envisioned the floodwaters rising so fast and high that they encompassed the entire first floors of buildings. Television images of people climbing into their attics, cutting holes in their roofs, waving for help, floating away—it was all daunting.

We tried to think of something we could do to help the victims other than just write a check. Fortunately, a ready opportunity arose. A horse-training facility near our Florida home was going to be housing hundreds of people displaced from the storm who would be bused there from New Orleans. They would stay in tiny dormitory-like apartments—glorified cubicles, really—usually reserved for exercise riders, grooms, muckers, and various other staff. And they would be coming with little more than the clothes on their backs, everything they owned having been swept up in the storm.

So we went into high gear, buying toothpaste, toothbrushes, socks, coffeepots, toasters, towels. We also went to every Costco, every Circuit City and Best Buy in Palm Beach County, to buy out their smaller televisions—somewhere between seventy and one hundred in all. It was the most important thing we could do. All people wanted was to get word of what was happening at home, and telephone systems were down in so many places. Phone systems weren't in the rooms yet, either. The facility was still pretty new. At least with television sets, people from New Orleans could watch the news and get updated, and maybe, if they were extremely lucky, catch a glimpse of a loved one still struggling at home.

We were fortunate to receive financial help from people in the show horse world when we asked for it. While we used tens of thousands of dollars of our own money, almost $20,000 poured in from friends and colleagues, helping to take the effort to the next level. Back and forth we went to the training facility in the Excursion, filled to the brim with supplies. We'd make a run, unload, go back home, pick up more stuff, and return to unload some more. Each drive back and forth from the house took about an hour.

After several days, when we finally finished, we kind of thought on one level, okay, we've done all we can. But we also knew we hadn't. People kept horses in and around New Orleans, and we felt we needed to do something to protect the animals. Our first notion was to take a few horses and bring them back to Beaver River Farm.

We made some calls and learned that those horses who managed to survive the hurricane had all been moved to outer parishes where the storm surge hadn't reached. They were okay. And people were already taking loads of hay and grain down so the horses wouldn't go hungry—they wouldn't be able to make use of feed that had been submerged in water. People were bringing medical supplies, too; a horse's skin starts to rot if it has been standing in water too long.

We were glad that the horse community had stepped up but at the same time were seeing disturbing images on television of dogs who had been caught in the mayhem. Newscasters started showing rescue workers picking up people in boats and taking them in helicopters from the tops of buildings, where they had climbed to escape the rising water. But the dogs were being left behind to balance by themselves on the rooftops—they weren't leaving with their human families. At that time there was no law in place, as there is now, that evacuees from storms and other emergency situations had the right to take their pets with them. (Hurricane Katrina was the impetus for that bill in the first place. The PETS Act, as it is called, was passed a year later, in 2006.)

It was hard to watch, and really left a sinking feeling in our stomachs. A person at least understands what is happening, even if it is scary, life-threatening. But a dog—a dog has no clue about why the waters are rising, or the speed of the wind, or the buildings falling apart. A dog doesn't understand why his human family is leaving him.

We saw so many images on television of dogs swimming for their lives, waiting to drown inside or on top of their abandoned houses, stuck on little islands formed by the ebb and flow of the floodwaters, stuck in trees. There were definitely good people in the maelstrom who were doing their level best to save them—throwing them ropes as lifelines, picking them up in rowboats or little motor boats, grabbing them from the water on catchpoles, long poles with a circle of rope tied to one end to scoop up a dog by the neck and bring him out of the deep water to safety.

But they weren't taking most of the dogs to shelters or homes. In the aftermath of the storm, with New Orleans ravaged, there simply weren't many places set up to accommodate them. So rescuers put the dogs in crates, in airline carriers and other types of travel bags, and took them to high ground in large warehouses, where they sat for weeks at a time with no food, no water, no care, no human touch. We read little snippets in the news that they were wallowing in their own waste, and starving at the same time.

Our adrenaline pumping, we knew we had to step into very high gear even though we were already very busy rescuing dogs in our free time. Whenever we were down in Florida, we'd go to the greyhound kennels and take some dogs who weren't running races anymore and were going to be put down, then find people to adopt them as pets. There's a misconception that greyhounds are going to be hyper dogs because they're such incredible runners, but they're actually the biggest couch potatoes you'll ever find, happy to lie around all day.

By the point at which we knew we had to help dogs after helping people, we were headed back to South Carolina after having set up the Florida house. Once we arrived home, we started by sending down dog supplies in our horse trailer—food, blankets, towels, newspapers, extra cages, dog shampoo—anything we could think of to help. But that wasn't enough. We had to get the dogs *out of there.*

So we developed a system whereby we'd send supplies down, and the horse trailer would come north with dogs. Since we were not a rescue organization but just two people who wanted to help, we ended up teaming with bona fide rescues and shelters that would vouch for us.

The first time, the trailer brought back almost three dozen dogs—big ones, little ones, brown ones, black ones, white ones, beige, yellow, multicolored, curly haired, smooth-furred, shaking, snarling, frightened, sweet-tempered, dazed. It would be easy to say that we felt at the moment entirely overwhelmed. Or relieved at having saved so many dogs and glad to be acting on every instinct we had been nourishing in ourselves since we were little. Or worried that we were in over our heads. And maybe we did feel some of those things, or all of them. But we had no time to sort through any of that. What we felt most of all was a great sense of urgency—more, even, than we had when taking the twenty-seven dogs from the condemned shelter near our house who had not been through a weather trauma.

They all needed to be (seriously) bathed, to go to the vet, to be walked, fed, acclimated, calmed down. All that was going through our minds was "We gotta help, we gotta help, we gotta help." It was a matter of just jumping into action. There was literally no time for thinking.

We weren't at all set up. There was a strong sense between us of "Oh my God, where are we going to put them all, and what if this one doesn't get along with that one?" And we had to buy more food bowls, and water bowls, and new fencing to create makeshift pens. It was a scramble with no opportunity for fore-thought.

Danny had begun putting fencing around his farm soon after he bought it in order to keep whatever dogs and horses he had rescued safe from coyotes and other animals, and also to keep the rescued animals from bolting. He had to make sure the thirty or so horses entrusted to his care for training by people who lived out of state were safely secured inside the boundary, too. But this was different. We could let some of the calmer, larger dogs loose at the farm because they were content to just hang out and find things that were interesting to them. Many liked to watch the far-rier on the days that he came to trim the horses' hooves and shoe them; they'd crowd around him like enthusiastic inspectors as he worked. But there were many dogs who were too sick and hungry to wander the acreage on their own. Or their fear and anxiety made them flight risks.

We needed to build pens where we could look after them, not just at the farm but also at the house we now shared. The makeshift pens we had created for the twenty-seven dogs from the shelter weren't going to be enough. We turned horse stalls into dog pens, too, as we had years earlier, and just let those horses who were temporarily removed from their stalls hang out in the pastures while the weather remained warm. We made room for some of the dogs in the smaller barn at Ron's house as well.

Once we cleaned the dogs up and got them to the vet, we learned that their medical care was going to be involved. Virtu-ally every single one of them tested positive for heartworm disease, which a dog can get from a single infected mosquito if not given preventive medicine (and there were plenty of mosquitoes in New Orleans in the moist aftermath of the storm). The worms live in the heart and can grow up to a foot in length, and the dogs needed to be treated with medication so the illness wouldn't get out of hand and make it too difficult to breathe.

They also needed all of their inoculations. There were no records on them, so everything had to be done from scratch—rabies vaccines, distemper shots, the whole panel of injections. Most of the dogs needed to be spayed or neutered, too, with the females requiring time to recuperate afterward. Spaying and neutering was critical. Even in the immediate aftermath of the storm, dogs wandering the streets of New Orleans were mating and creating new litters of homeless puppies. We whelped several litters of Katrina dogs ourselves when their pregnant mothers were driven north to us. Many were born unhealthy and needing special care because their mothers' nutritional and other health-care needs had not been met.

There was bandage changing as well, with a number of the dogs having sustained lacerations by being buffeted around and hit by who-knows-what in the fierce winds. We found ourselves in the position of critical-care nurses in an overflowing emergency room that consisted of our grounds and, in some instances, the house itself. A few dogs even had to learn how to be walked on a leash. It became clear to us that some of our canine refugees had not belonged to people but were feral, wandering the streets until they were picked up by animal rescuers taking them to warehouses.

Members of our staff who took care of the horses at Danny's farm helped with the dogs, but the cost of the care fell strictly upon us. We could not go back to our horse community after they had donated so generously for people who had been displaced to the horse-training facility in Florida. However, they were wonderful about taking dogs off our hands after they had been renourished and brought back to health. Many adopted a dog outright. Others would take three or four after we had rehabilitated them, and then get people to adopt them themselves.

But we were not even finished tending to that first batch of dogs when we realized we needed to remain all in. The scenes of struggling, abandoned dogs just kept coming.

Our horse trailer could hold about thirty-five dogs—even up to forty depending on their sizes. So we kept sending it down to New Orleans with supplies for equines that had been saved, and then it would come back loaded up with lost dogs, dropping off up to forty at a time—sometimes forty-one or forty-two if we pushed it.

We were not the only ones pitching in. "It wasn't like two little heroes just marched in and did this," Danny remarks. "This was hundreds and hundreds of people coordinating their efforts at shelters across the country to move dogs out of New Orleans. Like us, they knew that if they did not take them, they would be euthanized, and it was something they were trying desperately not to let happen. To think that most of these dogs came from loving homes and had their lives ripped out from under them— that was bad enough. But to then lose their lives because their owners no longer had the wherewithal to take care of them, no longer had a roof over their heads . . ."

We received deliveries of dogs more than twenty times in the months following the hurricane, with life becoming ever more frenetic. At times we had forty to fifty dogs at once in different stages of recovery—not yet to the doctor's; back from the doctor's and recuperating after a surgery or other procedure; afraid—of us, of the other dogs—and needing to be tended to separately, and gingerly. And then there were the odors—much worse than with the twenty-seven dogs from the shelter because of having sat for weeks on end in their crates in their own feces and urine. It would almost make us gag when we went to bathe them. Even after their initial baths, they still emitted an awful stench. It took many bathings over many weeks to get rid of the odor.

Then there were the dogs' medical needs. One of the most complicated and steepest medical learning curves thrown at us involved parvovirus. Like just about all other dog lovers, we had never been confronted with parvo before in our lives. That's because puppies are routinely inoculated against the disease by the time they are six to eight weeks old. But we received so many litters of very young puppies who had been born in the aftermath of the storm and had never received their standard vaccinations. And in many of those litters, every single dog had parvo—no surprise because it is highly contagious from pup to pup.

It's also a deadly illness, with nine out of ten dogs succumbing without prompt treatment. The virus attacks the gastrointestinal tract and immune system, causing severe vomiting and diarrhea as well as a secondary bacterial infection that spreads from the GI tract throughout the body.

We quickly had to learn about isolation so that a sick dog would not pass it to a healthy one, and also about disinfecting everything, including ourselves. We had to put our feet in bleach and wear janitors' jumpsuits to make sure we weren't facilitating the spread of the virus from one Katrina refugee to another. We also ended up taking a lot of the dogs for blood transfusions, and even so, lost a number of them.

On top of all of this, we were making runs to the airport to put this or that dog on a plane. People who had fallen in love with a photo put up online wanted to adopt a dog but lived halfway across the country and couldn't drive out to pick up their new pet.

We brought dogs to horse shows, too. We would rent stalls and, like carnival barkers, call out to people about the newly healthy, newly rehabilitated Katrina pets we were giving away. It was something of a hard sell. At that time people in the horse show world had a history of preferring purebred, pedigreed dogs, with different breeds going in and out of style—Yorkshire terriers, other little "fashion accessory" dogs, and so on. Even letting go of mongrels for free—clean, well-behaved mongrels but mongrels nonetheless—proved challenging.

With some six hundred dogs altogether coming into our care and needing new homes, we were not above putting people on the spot. One of them was Nora Thomas, a peer and a friend who also rode horses and trained riders. She already had an adorable but insecure Boston terrier named Francine and came to us when the dog was about a year old, saying that she felt like Francine needed a friend. This was before Katrina, but she knew we trafficked in rescue dogs and thought maybe we could find an appropriate match.

Once Katrina hit, we had plenty! We took some to the Pennsylvania Horse Show a couple of months after the storm hit, and, as Nora recalls it, "Ron comes up to me holding Phyllis, a beagle mix."

"Ron," Nora says she told him, "I'm a month away from getting married. Could it wait till after the wedding?"

"'Now, Nora,' Ron says to me, 'Hurricane Katrina didn't wait for Phyllis.'"

"I had never had a rescue dog prior to Phyllis," Nora relates. "I had always gotten my dogs from breeders and knew everything about them and their parents by the time I took them home. So she was kind of a mystery to me to figure out.

"The night we brought her back to the house, we put her in our camper with Francine for a couple of hours so we could go out to a dinner party that had already been arranged. When we came back, it was clear the two of them had had a party of their own. The curtains were all over the floor, the trash dumped out and completely gone through. I wondered what I was getting myself into.

"Then, when we were about to go on our honeymoon, I said to the young woman who would take care of things while we were away, 'Don't let Phyllis wander around the barn. I don't know what she'll get into.'

"Unbeknownst to me at the time, the minute my new husband and I left, both Phyllis and Francine found their way out to the barn, and from there Phyllis beelined for the field. She was missing for almost the entire six days we were away. The caretaker finally managed to catch up with her at a neighbor's house the day before we came back, a little dazed and world-weary but essentially okay.

"When we did arrive back home, I took Phyllis to the vet to be spayed. She was one of the few that Danny and Ron had not had spayed before offering her to me; they knew I would take proper care of her. 'Sorry,' the vet said. 'No doggie abortions at this stage.' I didn't know what he was talking about at first. But it turned out Phyllis was pregnant!

"She had the *cutest* litter of puppies. We couldn't keep them, but my accountant's sister works for the ASPCA, and they had a mini-telethon. All four puppies were adopted instantly.

"Poor Phyllis. She had such a rough start. But she became the . . . best . . . dog! And when my husband and I had our kids, first Harry and then Lil, she was always so kind and tolerant with them as babies and then toddlers and then grade schoolers, just so sweet and nice. I would never not do a rescue now. Those are the only dogs I take in."

The story of Nora and Phyllis is just one of many that had happy endings. But there were all kinds of hiccups in taking the dogs to the shows and trying to take care of them between events. Once, at the prestigious Deep Run Horse Show in Virginia, with many well-heeled attendees, we rented a few horse stalls to house eighteen dogs that we were trying to adopt out. We put signs on all the stalls: DO NOT OPEN DOORS. Any rescue dog could be a flight risk.

Don't you know, at almost eleven o'clock one night, after a fifteen-hour day, someone phoned our room and, when Ron picked up, said, "You're going to be very angry at me." We had no idea who she was.

"My children wanted to see the dogs, and they opened the stall doors . . . so all the dogs are loose."

Deep Run is situated in hunt country, where people go fox-hunting, so it's all wooded. That meant there were now eighteen dogs loose in the pitch-black forest night, running back and forth between the trees and the show grounds—and the roads that traversed the woods, which had us particularly worried. First we had to stop at Walmart to buy a bunch of flashlights, then we had to wake friends in the business who had already gone to bed for a dawn wake-up in order to get ready for the next day's happenings, to ask them if they'd come help us rescue the rescues.

We eventually caught sixteen of the far-flung dogs, but two remained missing even after three more hours of searching. They were particularly scared. By that point we were well into the wee hours and had to call it a night.

A little after daybreak, we finally saw the two of them running through the grounds. They kept making their way through rings and then from one ring to another, and neither we nor anybody else could catch them. Finally, we attached several of the dogs we had already recovered onto a lunge line, a very long line used to exercise horses. We then let the dogs loose on this long rope, and the two remaining runaways were intrigued enough that they ventured toward them and started playing with them. Ron kept reeling in the line, shorter and shorter, while the dogs continued to play, and when they got close enough, the two of us tackled them as if they were footballs. We managed to put all the dogs safely into the stalls, and then it was another full day of horse events.

The whole of the rescue effort was so helter-skelter, and we kept thinking we would have to stop, but how could we? So many of these Katrina dogs had been part of a family, secure, and then all of a sudden they're stuck in the noise of a howling wind that won't stop, with water all around them, in chaos, and they're put in crates in a dark warehouse to be euthanized if no one claims them, never being able to understand a thing that's going on.

And we were already part of a network. At one point someone even called us from Louisiana's official government offices and asked if we could take still more dogs. By that time we truly did think we had reached our breaking point—until we learned there were more dogs at risk of being put down for no other reason than that they had been caught in a storm.

Through all of this we continued doing our horse and rider training between shows. It wasn't like we could take a break of a few months from the work that paid our bills, and sometimes it meant putting in seventeen- to eighteen-hour days. There were people's horses that we kept at the farm who had to be tended to early in the morning, training facilities where we needed to meet various clients and their horses. All this was in addition to horse shows we had committed to out of town—which meant hiring someone for a night or two to at least feed all the dogs and make sure they got outside to do their business. (The woman who didn't like mice had long before stopped coming by.) When we'd arrive back home, it was back to giving flea baths to newly arrived dogs, playing with them and training them as much as possible, feeding them, dispensing medications . . . Many times it felt impossible. But impossible wasn't acceptable. "If we had to put in more hours, we put in more hours," Ron says. "Whatever had to be done, we got done."

Sometimes a single dog required nearly all our energy, like the miniature dachshund who was delivered as part of a particularly large shipment of some forty-five dogs. The moment we removed her from the crate, she backed out of her collar and took off. We started running after her, but it was clear that wasn't going to work—even a little dog can run a good fifteen miles an hour—so Ron jumped in his car and started following her. No luck.

"I remember coming back and seeing Danny and just looking at him," Ron says. "I welled up in tears. 'We're never going to find this dog.'" She was so frightened, not knowing us from a hole in the wall, lost out in the woods more than seven hundred miles from her original home.

Darkness set in as we went about the business of taking care of the other new arrivals, plus dogs we'd already had on the property a while and hadn't adopted out yet. We left the porch light on as well as the floodlights at the side of the house.

At about one in the morning, Ron started to think he was hearing little "yip" sounds. "I kind of lay on my pillow, falling in and out of sleep, thinking I had it wrong. But then I heard the 'yip' again, and it was indisputable. I woke Danny, and we started looking out the bedroom windows."

There she was. We knew that if we went out the front door she was going to take off again. But where she was standing near the front of the house, there was a horse pasture that had wire mesh fencing around three sides—she wouldn't be able to get through it. The fourth side had just split-rail fencing, however. She could easily go through. So we made a plan to close it off.

Just before sunrise, we got out of bed and went downstairs and out the back door. As we suspected she would, the dog came around from the front to the back and started barking at us, then ran into that pasture. There really weren't any other options for her. A clump of trees with wild rose bushes mixed in stood in the middle of the pasture, and we could see her go straight into that thicket.

Immediately, according to plan, we went and opened the garage door and grabbed everything we could to fill in the spaces in the 200-foot length of split-rail fencing—hay bales, quilts, horse blankets, crates, tarps, baskets—everything we could find that wouldn't allow her to jump through or walk under the rails. We had to race to put it all in place. "It looked like a gypsy caravan" with all the blankets and other paraphernalia, Danny says.

Back into the middle of the pasture we went after we "reinforced" the fence. The little dog was barking and snarling at us from the clump of trees. Ron took a broom with a little screw eye at its end and made a kind of lasso configuration from hay twine, running the line through the screw and then back to himself. It was kind of like the catchpoles in New Orleans that we had seen on TV.

From the border of the thicket, "The dog was literally snapping at us like an alligator," Ron recalls. Danny kept aggravating her to distract her so Ron could get alongside her and push the lasso over her head. Once he retrieved her, he held her as close to his body as he could so she wouldn't be able to start biting. Danny opened a dog crate, and we managed to secure her.

That night, after a good bath, she did a complete one-eighty and slept between us under the covers, her head literally on one of our pillows. We named her Lucy.

We were thoroughly exhausted from having been up much of the night before—and clearly in way over our heads—and, through our fatigue, energized and exhilarated. *This was working.* We were taking desperate dogs destined to lose their lives and making them happy, secure, adoptable. We were rehabilitating them to become dogs that belonged in people's homes.

But there was much we weren't doing right—or as carefully as would have been good for the dogs. We were so desperate to get each one placed that we didn't know where a lot of them ended up. If a friend from the horse community took a few and "distributed" them, we didn't know who the dogs' new families were or whether they would make a good fit. We didn't know if the dogs were just going to be fostered for a while at someone's home and then be adopted by a forever family. If someone adopted a dog from the other side of the country, we didn't have the time to conduct an in-depth interview with them to see if they had children; some dogs don't get on well with toddlers or young school-age kids. We weren't able to determine if they had a big fenced-in yard for dogs who would bolt once let off the leash but still needed a place to romp.

We figured anyone who would go through the trouble of adopting a homeless dog who had been through a hurricane had the best intentions and would certainly try their hardest to give their new pet a good life. But the lack of knowledge nagged at us.

And frustratingly, we had virtually zero success in reuniting dogs with their original families, even though it was understandable. People's lives had been completely upended. They had no home, no job, not even a single item from their lives before the hurricane, as we knew from getting supplies to the horse-training center. No family photos, high school graduation diplomas, marriage licenses, or anything else that would have had sentimental or practical value. So the last thing they were going to be able to do was try to reclaim their pet.

Even if they wanted to find their dog, it wasn't going to be easy—or possible. At that time, social media wasn't where it is today. Facebook had only started a year earlier. Twitter and Instagram didn't even exist. There was no one place online where it was possible to share information with large numbers of people. There were just some on-the-fly websites that people had created to try to reconnect people with their pets, and coming across your dog on one of those sites was a long shot at best, as we well knew from posting dogs on them.

That meant unclaimed dogs would go off to new households—members of our horse community, people all over the country. One little dog named Skipper, the sweetest black Pomeranian, was one of those destined for the canine diaspora. We knew he had belonged to someone, because he was just so chipper, so co-operative, so eager and pleasant to be around. And we posted his photo online, but to no avail.

Fortunately, a lovely family in Buffalo, New York, decided to adopt him. Somebody we knew happened to be flying there and would take him under the seat.

But the day before the flight, his New Orleans family reached out to us. They had resettled in Houston, as so many Katrina families did, and had been worried sick about their dog. They posted a photo of him that they had managed to hold on to, and sure enough, it was Skipper. We were amazed to find his picture on one of the lost-pet websites.

The Buffalo people completely understood and were thrilled for Skipper to be able to go back to his "real" family. Better still, they were happy to take another dog in his place.

Out of all the hundreds of dogs we managed to rescue after the storm, Skipper was the only one we were able to reunite with the people who had to evacuate without their pet. We have no photos of Skipper ourselves—the site was long ago taken down—and don't even remember the family's name. The swirl of the hurricane was followed by the swirl of our own activity and the swirl of survivors adjusting to their new lives. Nobody was thinking to preserve those moments for posterity. We and many others were glad so many dogs were saved from death, but if only Skipper's reunification with his people could have been the fate for more of the dogs.

In some cases, that wouldn't have been possible no matter what. Toward the very end of the ordeal, when we were already well past the middle of November and were now taking our last "delivery," two dogs, the first black and tan, the second charcoal-colored, came to us huddled together in a single crate. The charcoal dog seemed to have a bit of greyhound in her, and the other, some other type of hound. Taped to the top of the crate was a note: "Please keep Milly and Daisy together." They were found floating on a dining room table, their owner, an elderly woman, on the floor next to them, drowned in the rising waters.

In the wake of Hurricane Katrina, Milly *(left)* and Daisy were found floating together in a single crate on a dining room table with a note attached asking to keep them together. Their owner was lying on the floor next to them, drowned in the rising waters.

Chapter 4

Unanticipated Houseguests

By the time the ordeal of Katrina ended, we had pretty much depleted all our savings. This included cashing in much of the retirement funds that we had saved over decades, absorbing a stiff pre-withdrawal penalty in the process. But what we lost in funds, we gained in dogs! Prior to the hurricane, we always had some of our own pet dogs in the house with us, along with maybe a few others that we were hoping to adopt out. But many of the ones we rescued from shelters each month who were already on the list to be euthanized, along with those we found at the side of the road, stayed in outdoor pens or the horse stalls, just like most of the Katrina dogs.

Now we had some fifteen to twenty dogs in the house all at once. Yes, we had managed to place almost six hundred canine refugees from the storm, but some were simply not yet adoptable. Having been through more than the dogs we had taken from the local shelter years earlier, they were still too scared to become someone's pet and were apt to lash out aggressively or just cower miserably. Some had seemingly never been around people before and needed a whole other level of acclimation. They had probably been feral dogs on the streets of New Orleans and got scooped up with those pets who had been separated from their human families in the mass rescues.

Then there were some who were never going to be able to live with other people no matter what—or who we simply weren't going to be able to part with. That was the case with Milly and Daisy. We felt they had simply been through too much trauma. They clearly were insecure, and we couldn't bear to cut the tie we had made with them and upend their lives all over again.

And they definitely couldn't be separated from each other.

Besides, they were, for lack of a better word, strange. "Milly never learned to tote a full seed bag," as Danny puts it. "If you even just looked at her too intensely, she'd run away."

She also had an unusual, involved ritual for relieving herself. She would come out of the bedroom, make precisely four laps around the living room, run back into the bedroom, jump up on one side of the bed, off the opposite side, and then repeat the entire process—three or four times before finally making her way outside. If you called to her during this procedure, she would crawl under the bed and refuse to come out; you could see her white eyelashes arcing over her peering eyes while her charcoal-black body faded in the darkness under the mattress. We learned not to try to coax her. You had to let her go through her special liturgy without interruption.

She sometimes slept on the bed with us, but only according to a very prescribed protocol. For one thing, she would never lie on the bed until we were already tucked in, quiet and still. She would position herself between our two pairs of feet. And once other dogs climbed onto the bed after we were all settled, she would go to sleep on the couch with Daisy—although as she aged, we sometimes also found her at the foot of the bed when we awoke in the morning. But she never became a dog that you could just decide to go and pet and shower with affection. She was tentative even about a casual stroking or petting. "She wanted to be near you, but not exactly with you," Danny says. Adds Ron, "Till the day she died, there was no yearning for human touch." She wore her anxiety on her body. As taut as a whippet at thirty-five pounds, she always stayed extremely lean.

Eighty-five-pound Daisy, whose confidence Milly depended on to keep her safe, fared better. She was bigger than any dog we had ever planned on keeping in the house full-time; we thought it would make things much harder for all the little dogs who had washed up on our doorstep in the wake of Katrina. And, hound mix that she was, she would bark incessantly at feeding time and get into squabbles with the other dogs, so she had to be put into her crate while they ate. But other than that, she was very generous with her space. And she learned to love everybody in her environment, dogs and people alike. She became a veritable cuddle buddy.

The one thing that would send her into a true emotional tailspin was bad weather. Both she and Milly, in fact, would become frantic at the prospect of a storm. And they knew before anyone else that one was coming. There could be blue skies but the two of them would start panting, and soon after, a massive thundercloud would roll in overhead and the torrent would begin. Maybe the other dogs knew ahead of time, too, but Daisy's and Milly's memories of rain and wind and loss and displacement had made a deeper impression. It was so bad that the only time Milly would cling to us was right before wet weather began. We called the two of them our weather girls. They did a better job than the meteorologists on TV.

While Milly and Daisy's story haunted us because of the note left in their crate, each dog taken into in our care after Katrina had particular needs, especially as they all had been through an ordeal. That was fine in our book. After a lifetime of perhaps belonging to someone and having their entire existence upended, we were happy to provide them with a home and security till the end of their days, if they needed.

We probably couldn't have articulated it at the time, but with each of us knowing firsthand what it felt like not to belong, to feel insecure about our place in our own families, we were not about to turn away any sentient beings who needed love and acceptance for who they were. It may have been a subconscious imperative, but it was a pressing one nonetheless.

Still, it became clear to us that we had to hire someone in a serious way to help us take care of the new dogs in our charge. After all, we were often away at horse shows and couldn't continue to depend on the kindness of the groomsmen and other equine professionals who helped us out at the stables—or the young woman named Karen Odom who would come to stay at the house in our absence. And even when we were there, we didn't have enough hands for fifteen to twenty dogs—especially dogs with special needs.

It was going to mean spending more money that we didn't really have to spend, not just on the outside help but also on all the extra food and medical care. We were not a formal rescue—you couldn't make a donation to our effort and use it as a tax write-off. So everything was out of pocket. We never even considered charging a few hundred dollars for adoptions, as formal rescues often do, in order to help them recoup the costs of vaccinations, deworming, spaying and neutering, and other medical care. To us it was an honor just that anyone was *willing* to give one of these dogs a new home. To cover costs, Ron took out a home equity line of credit—a second mortgage.

The term "home equity" struck us as ironic, because while people often take out second mortgages to make repairs to their houses, *this* loan was all about tending to a new batch of canines who were accelerating our home's disrepair. The hardwood floors were reaching their end—rotting out from urine, from canine nails scratching through the polyurethane finish. To resurface them would have required that we sand them down, restain them, and put on four new coats of polyurethane. It wasn't going to happen, not just because it's impossible to do all that with a couple dozen dogs in the house, but also because it was an expense we couldn't take on.

As for the oriental rugs, we finally rolled them up. "They were being peed on, chewed on," Danny says. "The easiest solution was no more rugs."

The fronts and backs of all the doors were now scratched up, too, from dogs trying to make their way from one room to another. We screwed plexiglass onto them so the animals wouldn't be able to continue to rip and destroy the wood.

The furniture underwent further wear and tear as well. We resorted to spraying the couches and chairs with pet store sprays that had odors designed to turn dogs off and keep them away— sour apple, hot pepper—and when that didn't work, placing couch covers and chair covers on the seating to protect the leather. And when *that* didn't work, using rolls and rolls of black duct tape to fill in holes and prevent more stuffing from escaping the fabric and forming little clouds all over the house.

We lost a lot of lamps, too, adding to the financial toll. The dogs would try to jump on an end table or knock against one as they ran by, and a lamp would fly off and shatter. We started buying lamps made of metal instead of glass. We also had to make sure to cover the cords that went from outlets *to* the lamps. The dogs seemed to have a penchant for trying to chew through anything that could a) hurt them, b) cause an electrical short, or c) create a direct fire hazard.

Finally, we ended up purchasing a number of crates that we outfitted with soft blankets and plush toys, learning that some dogs actually felt more secure with a "room of their own" rather than roaming around the house. It necessitated moving furniture around and crowding in spaces that formerly had open sight lines and plenty of elbow room. Our home was becoming more and more the dogs' home.

But the education we were getting you couldn't put a price on. We could see even better than we had been able to at first that, living with us as part of our family, rescue dogs who had weathered a storm, literally, had an opportunity to become calmer, less difficult, than is often possible in a shelter. In the institutionalized setting of a shelter, it's hard for a dog to come to be his or her best self. It's not that shelter staff don't work very hard to do their best by the animals in their care. But living in a shelter is simply not the same as living in a home—jumping on the bed at will, wandering about freely and playing with other dogs whenever the mood strikes, coming to you for attention when ready, sitting on someone's lap and watching television while getting stroked on the muzzle, greeting people when they come to the door . . . With those freedoms, even a traumatized dog can become the dog he's supposed to be.

We have actually seen this over and over through the years. A dog starts out at our house either hiding under a chair or ready to lash out aggressively if you go near him, because he is afraid you would try to hurt him. Then he'll work his way out a little bit and start following some of the other dogs. They all go out the doggy door together and farther and farther into the yard.

Or we'll see a dog come to the bedroom one night and stare at us and then run out the door. And then, maybe two weeks later, he'll make it to the edge of the bed. Not on the bed but just to the bed, and then he'll shoot out the door again. Then he'll make it to the edge of the bed and let you reach down and pet him before running out. Finally, after a few more weeks, he'll climb onto the bed—maybe by making his way up the little set of stairs that we put to the side of the mattress for the dogs who are too small to jump up—and stay in a corner, near our feet. And jump off if you move toward him.

At some point he'll graduate from that perch, snuggling right next to one of us for warmth and closeness. *That's* a dog someone wants to adopt. Over time, on his own terms, he acclimates to being with people and comes to prefer the company of humans instead of fearing them because he is unused to them or because someone may have once hurt him or neglected him or because he has been through unimaginable terror and separation anxiety.

The Katrina dogs were our initial proof of this, and not only did many of them calm down, but their living right in the house with us also bought time to teach them how to walk on a leash, if necessary, and for them to learn cues for such things as going into their crates or taking their medicine. We even learned that with time we could come to understand dogs' different personalities and so match the right dog with the right adopter.

In one instance, the adopter was Danny's sister Cheryl. While we still had some Katrina dogs left, we were driving down a country road one day—we had popped in the CD of *The Lion King*—and saw an emaciated dog on the other side, down in a gully. "I mean skeleton," Ron says. We had to drive past him and find a side road to make a U-turn, then followed the ditch in the other direction until we eyed him again.

He wouldn't come to us. We spent about twenty minutes sitting at the top of the gully's bank at the edge of the road, calling to him and trying to cajole him into trusting us enough to let us get near him. The scary part was his panicking every time he heard a car approaching. We worried that in his fear, the dog would dart out in front of the vehicle to try to reach the other side of the road.

Finally, when it became all too clear that our cooing entreaties were going to do no good, we pulled an old breakfast bag from the car, maybe from Hardee's or Wendy's or some other place we had stopped for biscuits, and started shaking it. His ears turned, but that was it. A full twenty more minutes of coaxing went by until he finally started crawling to us on his belly. We had scared the poor dog into a combat maneuver.

But the bag retained enough of a scent that he eventually came right up to it to sniff, and it was at that point that we put a collar over his head that was attached to a leash. We have always carried extra leashes in the car for scenarios just like that one.

Even though he was still a puppy, he was a rather large, rangy thing, black and tan, some kind of hound mix. Up close, the dog smelled to high heavens. And he was full of fleas and ticks, with big patches of hair missing—made you kind of sick to your stomach.

We put him in the back of the car and opened all the windows to help with the odor, and it was at that point, when we could look him in the face, that we could see how sweet he was, with big expressive eyes that kind of reminded us of Goofy. Except Goofy looked healthy, and this dog just looked sad. Who knows what he had been through? If only they could tell you.

Once we arrived home, we put him in the yard, and he immediately had to go potty. But surprisingly, his stool had all these bright colors in it—bright whites and oranges and reds and yellows. He had been eating wrappers from all the fast food joints that people throw onto the side of the road and still have biscuit and hamburger grease on them, that's how hungry he was.

We took him to the vet, who put his age at about three months, and it turned out he had pancreatitis—a condition in which the enzymes of the pancreas start eating away at the pancreas itself. It can occur in a dog who has eaten more fat than is good for him. He had to spend several days at the vet's because he was dehydrated and needed fluid intravenously and was also weak from frank anemia.

"We had to get his blood count back up," Ron explains. "The fleas and ticks had taken so much blood out of him. We couldn't even initially get him the necessary vaccines because his health was so fragile."

When we finally were able to bring him home, he was so submissive it was pitiful. He would assume a crouched position any time you tried to talk to him or pet him. "It wasn't like he was shaking in his boots," Danny says. "He just didn't know how to act in front of someone who was liking him instead of hating him."

"He was a broken soul," Ron adds, "very withdrawn, very depressed, and in a deep dark place."

"It really made your heart hurt," Danny says. "His tail would give a little wag over to this side, and then slowly over to that side, and then back over to the first side again. It was like a metronome going so slowly it looked like it would just stop."

We named him Simba, hoping he would be able to take his rightful place as a proud dog, a loved dog, like the main character of *The Lion King*, which cued his discovery.

The first thing we had to do was start getting good nutrition into him. He was fairly calm, but that was in large part because he was still so drained physically. We were thinking that as he began to feel better, he would perk up, and he did, but at first, his perking up was alarm. He would react more than other dogs to noises, hand movements, anything sudden. It made him startle, and he would have to look at us and decide if things were okay or if we were going to abuse him. He was still haunted by old skeletons.

Simba kept away from the other dogs, too. He just didn't want any trouble. Even little Buttercup, the papillon Ron adopted from the shelter the moment her owner had haughtily given her up and who took all the comings and goings of dogs with aplomb, couldn't jolly him out of his sadness. But after a while, as he learned that he could trust us, and as his emotional health began to catch up with the advances in his physical health, his tail began to wag with a little more alacrity. A spark began to replace the solemnity in his eyes.

He even became playful, romping and wrestling with the other dogs. He remained clumsy for a while—all legs and big feet, like a Disney dog. But as he grew out of his illness, he learned how to control his body.

He never got into fetching and retrieving things, but he loved carrying soft toys—a little teddy bear, a small stuffed animal monkey. "Look what I have," his expression would say, his tail wagging. He was very proud of his acquisitions and would bring them to you to start a tug-of-war.

We happily indulged him. You can't play tug-of-war with a dog who's maybe a little too big for his britches and needs some solid leadership, but for a dog you're trying to coach out of his shell, it's the perfect game. Letting a dog win imbues him with confidence.

That confidence allowed him to start coming over to us more and more, to seek our attention rather than fear it. In fact, by the time we knew he was ready to be adopted, he was following us around the house, sitting with us as we watched TV. He even learned to love sitting in our laps on the couch, but he grew so fast that that didn't last for long. He kept trying for a while but realized on his own that he wasn't going to be able to get comfortable and settled for just coming over to rest his chin on one of our knees. In the space of just two and a half to three months, he went from wanting to keep away to wanting to be physically connected as much as possible.

We thought he'd make a perfect addition to Danny's sister Cheryl's house. Cheryl already had Leafy, a schnauzer cross with what seemed like some sort of spaniel mixed in—kind of fat with a wiry gray coat and short legs that supported her chunky body. Leafy got along with everybody, but what was important for Cheryl was not having a second dog who was going to be so high-energy that he'd prove hyper. Simba fit the bill. He was engaged and had a sweet temperament but was not the type of dog who bounced off the walls. Cheryl also didn't mind the idea of a big hound who looked a bit more imposing than Leafy and would sound a little more intimidating when someone knocked on the door and he would bark in response.

Our intuition was right. Cheryl loved Simba, and Simba and Leafy got on famously. They'd chase each other through the house, then lie down together on a big cushion that Cheryl left on the floor. They *always* slept together, in fact. Simba essentially became Leafy's big brother, even though Leafy had been there first.

Over time, we were able to adopt out most of the Katrina holdovers as well, even though we held on to Milly and Daisy. With some it took more effort—different dogs, like different people, have different capacities for resilience, and some need more time to come around. But come around most of them did—both with their physical health and their psychological well-being. We were thrilled at this chance to rehabilitate so many dogs who might not otherwise have had a chance.

Our accountant, not so much. "You're bleeding money," he said, exasperated as he went over our expenses. "You're going to have to retire someday. Have you thought about that?"

* * *

If someone did not take Elmer, the shelter was going to have to put him down. He had urgent medical needs that they could not afford to tend.

When we finally got a look at the miniature long-haired dachshund, his eyes had a kind of opaque milkiness to them. And they were filled with yellow pus that kept crusting over. He could hardly see. But that wasn't the worst of it.

His jaw had several fractures that made his teeth stick out sideways from his mouth at a 90-degree angle instead of going straight up and down like they were supposed to. Someone had beaten him with their fists or perhaps thrown him out of a car—we never found out which. But it was so bad that his lip actually scalloped upward. The misaligned teeth had eaten away at the skin that should have allowed his mouth to close; it remained perpetually open. He also had a handgun bullet lodged in his abdomen.

Unable to chew, Elmer was emaciated. He could get down some soft food, but it was difficult because his tongue perpetually hung out the side of his mouth—there was no place to put it.

What killed us was that he was so happy and trusting, wagging his tail all the time and glad to be held, petted, or cooed over by the two of us and everyone else. He had every right to hate all of humanity; he didn't know he deserved better.

We figured he'd need surgery to repair his teeth, but it went way beyond that. Dogs have a series of small bones that go across the roof of the mouth, covered by tissue. But the tissue—the palate—was gone, so much of the food he managed to take in was going up through the roof of his mouth and coming out of his nose. It was as if he had a completely cleft palate.

He ended up needing seven surgeries. Some, but not all of

them, were to have the roof of his mouth rebuilt, with skin grafts and all the rest. And the grafts didn't always take, so they'd have to be repeated.

He also had to have nearly all of his teeth extracted. There was no fixing them. It wasn't just that they had been so blown out of kilter. They were caked with dark yellowish brown tartar—he had experienced not only straight-up abuse but also years of neglect. You couldn't even see his actual teeth, in fact. They looked like misshapen rocks.

On top of all that, Elmer needed operations on both of his eyes. We thought for sure he'd be blind, but he did not lose his sight.

After $23,000 in operating procedures, he was finally out of pain, with his vision much improved. But who was going to adopt this dog ravaged by cruelty, who was already at least ten years old? Who was going to be willing to tend to his continued need for intensive medical care?

It turned out a young woman who worked for our rescue at the time, Val Evans, was completely besotted with him. "I was the only one that Elmer let do his eye drops," Val says. "It had to be three or four times a day. He had dry eye but also, because he was not able to chew and could only use his tongue, he lost muscle mass in the top of his head, so his eye sank in. They tried to correct the problem by bringing his eye forward during one of the surgeries, but his heart rate dipped so low they had to get him off the anesthesia before they could address it. He was lucky to make it off the table that day.

"I started to come in on my days off to take care of him. I'd end up staying all day because I had to keep giving him the drops at periodic intervals. There were other things, too. It turned out he had heartworm disease and also needed treatment for that. And I had to keep him calm during the treatment because he could throw a clot if he got worked up over anything. A dog on heartworm meds can't be getting all excited.

"I think it was around then that I knew I would adopt him. There was a lot going on in my life personally. I was in a relationship that was becoming more and more serious, and I figured I was going to be undergoing some pretty big life changes, but it had reached the point that Elmer and I couldn't be away from each other.

"He should have hated the human race because of what happened to him, but he loved snuggling up with me. And he's super protective. Even though he weighs ten pounds, he thinks he's the toughest guy on earth. It took him a while to accept that my boyfriend was on the scene."

But Val's boyfriend and Elmer did finally make their peace with each other, so much that Elmer was a member of their wedding party—a groomsman extraordinaire.

Today both Val and her husband, Brian Moore, are together so devoted to Elmer that even though Brian is currently stationed in New Mexico as a US Air Force captain, Val has remained behind in South Carolina so that Elmer can continue to have his ongoing veterinary care at home (courtesy of Danny & Ron's Rescue). He still has a lot of medical issues. There are literal holes in both his cheeks from where surgeons removed cheek area to save his life when they were taking care of his mouth, so he continues to be prone to infection. He also continues to have oral-nasal fistulas— holes in the roof of his mouth that can't close up. Some of them had been closed with sutures, but they kept popping open until the doctors decided it was better to stop putting him through more surgeries. And because of his sunken eye, his eyelid finally had to be removed because it kept rolling onto his eyeball (the condition is called entropion) and causing severe irritation.

But at thirteen he remains a happy dog and was even named "Military Pet of the Year" by an organization called Dogs on Deployment. His incredible survival story garnered him the votes on social media.

"The platform of Dogs on Deployment is about the value of canine rescue," Val says. "But it's also that your scars don't define you. You may struggle, but there is still life out there, and it's going to get better."

Of course, Elmer never knew what all the fuss was about when he had his photo snapped with Val's husband, Captain Moore. He just knew he was well loved and taken care of. He continues to lead a good life, never knowing why he was mistreated or why he was then loved and well cared for. Dogs have no agency in their fate. It is up to us.

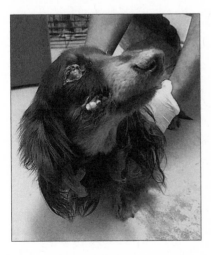

Elmer before: Someone had beaten Elmer with their fists or perhaps thrown him out of a car—we never found out which. He also had a bullet lodged in his abdomen.

Elmer after: Seven surgeries later, 10-year-old Elmer was finally out of pain. After he was adopted by Val Evans, he became "best man" at her wedding to US Air Force Captain Brian Moore and even went on to receive the distinction of "Military Pet of the Year" by an organization called Dogs on Deployment.

Chapter 5

Heart Breaking

Money worries would have to wait. Gadget, Flo, Tillie, and Trifles all piled into the Ford Excursion with us for the three-hour trip to Raleigh, North Carolina. We were going to stay at our good friend George's apartment while we worked the annual Jump for the Children charity horse show, which raised funds for the Children's Hospital at Duke University. It was always a grand time. We enjoyed seeing George, and the four dogs, Jack Russell terriers all, loved getting together with "Uncle George's" dog Norman, also a Jack Russell who happened to be a grandson of Moonpie—the dog Danny had when he bought Beaver River Farm. It was a regular Jack Russell–palooza. The dogs jumped all over one another in delight at first greeting and loved coming to the horse show with us and driving around in the golf cart. At night, Trifles, who was getting on in years, would sleep on the floor while the rest of the dogs climbed onto our bed or George's.

Our first night there, Danny passed out at the bathroom sink around 4 a.m. Ron did not hear the thud.

Danny had actually felt very uncomfortable throughout the night. He was "up and down, up and down, kind of fidgety," Ron says. "It was as though he didn't know what to do with himself. He kept saying he felt really funny. He couldn't stop pacing."

Ron repeatedly asked Danny if there was anything he could do for him, but Danny said no. Finally, Ron fell into a deep sleep before the long day ahead of them. Danny got out of bed in the wee hours because the house had only one bathroom, and he needed extra time to put on his riding clothes before we left for the stables.

When he came to after falling, he crawled back to the bed and curled up in a fetal position on the floor, calling out to Ron that he felt like he had a shield on his chest. "It's just so hot—burning," he said. "I feel like I'm burning up from the inside."

Ron's first thought was that Danny was having a heart attack. "His voice had been hoarse for a long time," Ron explains. "I had been having a funny feeling something wasn't right. And now this."

Ron woke George to say he was going to take Danny to the hospital. But by this time it was already 5 a.m., and Ron was supposed to be at the horse show by 5:30. There were some thirty horses that he had to ready for the day's events. George told Ron that *he* would get Danny to the hospital while Ron got things going at the horse show. "You know all your clients," George said. "I won't be able to get the ball rolling for you."

"I didn't like that idea," Ron says, "but it wasn't like a television kind of heart attack where people grab their chests and are gone. Danny was still walking, still verbal. I thought maybe it could even be an ulcer. So while I was frightened, I listened to George, figuring I'd go get things started at the show and then rush over to the hospital. It was only a five-minute drive."

But things didn't work out that way. Ron had barely gotten started at the show grounds—flipping through the schedule, seeing if he could get any friends to ride some of the horses Danny was supposed to ride—when George called from the emergency room and told Ron he needed to come over immediately.

As soon as Danny and George had arrived at the emergency room, George explained what had happened, saying that Danny really needed to be seen immediately. The triage unit saw it differently, deciding that Danny needed to wait in line. But then he dropped to the floor again, which is when the medical staff jumped into action.

In the meantime, Ron raced to the hospital.

"Who are you?" the doctor asked when Ron rushed in, asking to get right over to Danny in the intensive care unit.

"I'm his partner," Ron responded.

The doctor hesitated for a moment, then said, "Your friend is in very, very serious condition." It turned out Danny had an aortic aneurysm that was dissecting—his aorta was literally shredding apart—and there was nothing that could be done to stop it.

The aorta is the critical blood vessel from which the heart pumps out blood to all the body's organs. It consists of three layers, and two of those layers were tearing up. A weakness in the aorta—the aneurysm—was responsible. The doctor was blunt.

"Most people die within four hours," he said. "Your friend has a ten percent chance of making it." The actor John Ritter had died suddenly of an aortic dissection stemming from an undiagnosed aneurysm.

Ron felt like his blood was dropping from his head to his feet. He immediately started crying. "People fall in love," he says. "I definitely fell in love with Danny. I loved everything about him, and we shared so many of the same passions and interests in life, including our feelings about animals. But people fall out of love, too. The thing is, as our love grew it taught me that Danny was my soul mate on this earth. And you can't fall out of soul mate. I felt like I couldn't breathe myself, like someone was pushing on my own chest. I didn't try to imagine what it would be like to live without him. I wouldn't let myself go there."

After that the doctor refused to talk anymore to Ron or let him make any decisions. He was not Danny's next of kin, and the law prohibited his involvement in Danny's medical treatment. It was 2007, we had not had a wedding ceremony, and gay marriage had not yet been recognized in any state other than Massachusetts, anyway.

We had papers making each the other's health-care proxy for just such an incident as this, but those papers were at home in South Carolina, and Ron would not be able to produce them on the spot. "They were telling me Danny could die at any moment but that I couldn't know what was going on or weigh in on any avenue of treatment," Ron says. "They treated me like I was a stranger to him.

"Everybody experiences a medical emergency in life. It's scary and emotional, and that's bad enough. But then the frustration of being told, 'You have no agency in this situation unless you can produce documents . . .' I felt like I had a gun to my head. Every second counted. If I were a woman and walked in and said I was Mrs. Robertshaw, they wouldn't have batted an eyelash or asked me to prove it by showing them documentation. They would have told me everything I needed to know and run all choices and decisions by me."

Ron called Danny's sisters. He was going to call them in short order, anyway—they needed to come see their brother, perhaps for the last time. And they were like family to Ron as well. "Danny's sisters were always wonderful to me," Ron says. "I was very blessed that way." But now their involvement became critical.

The doctors in the intensive care unit wanted to put an arterial line into Danny to deliver medicines into his body as quickly as possible. Danny's sisters, Cheryl and Lynne, got on the phone with one of the doctors and said that they could say anything in front of Ron and also that whatever decisions he made were fine. But it wasn't enough. They had to come and sign an affidavit in person. And they were almost three hours away in Wilmington, North Carolina. It was going to take them a while to reach the hospital.

In the meantime, Ron was trying frantically to reach someone taking care of the rescue dogs back home in South Carolina who could rifle through his papers, find the signed living will and health-care proxy documents, and fax them over. He finally did, but the hospital still wanted Danny's sisters to sign an affidavit saying that Ron was allowed to hear updates on Danny's prognosis and also to make medical decisions.

"I understood the legality," Ron says. "Doctors can get sued. But still, it felt so cold, so heartless. The person you love is on death's doorstep—you don't want to be pushed out because of legal technicalities."

Finally, an arterial line *was* put in, and Danny was also put into a medically induced coma. The aorta continued to shred, and his body needed to stay as quiet and still as possible if there was any chance that the tearing would ease off.

Ron sat fitfully in the waiting room that night with periodic updates. "Sitting out in that lobby, every time I watched the doors open, the pit in my stomach would grow larger," he says.

One of the doctors told him curtly, "He's either going to live, or he's going to die," before walking back through the doors and into the intensive care unit.

It was not until just before dawn the next morning that the aorta ceased tearing any further. But Danny was nowhere near out of the woods. At that point the rip stretched from his heart to all his abdominal organs. It was pretty much the longest dissected aorta any cardiologist had ever seen, and the hope against hope was that the third layer of his aorta wouldn't give way, too. That would kill him instantly.

A little later that morning, Ron and Danny's sisters, who had arrived by that point, went down to the hospital cafeteria to get a little food into them. At Danny's level of intensive care, a nurse would be at his bedside 24/7, so they knew he would be in good hands for the half hour or so that they'd be gone. But when they walked back into the room, the walls and ceiling were covered in blood; blood was literally spraying all over the place. They feared the worst.

But what happened was that Danny had woken a little from his induced coma and pulled out the arterial line. A nurse was not in the room at the time.

"I was so scared—and very angry," Ron says. He immediately ran to get someone, and they put pressure on the artery to stop the bleeding and reinserted the line.

"It was a very emotional journey," Ron comments. "After a few days, Danny's sisters had to leave, get back to their lives, although they'd come on the weekends. I was basically there by myself. I spent probably twenty hours a day at the hospital. I'd go back to George's apartment just to shower and change before returning to the hospital to sleep in a chair by Danny's bed.

"The dogs, of course, were completely befuddled. They were used to *always* being with us when we took that trip—both at George's and at the horse show. It was clear they were missing Danny and me, because when I'd come in, they'd run over to me wiggling and waggling as usual, but with a 'Where have you been?' demeanor. No doubt their concern was only heightened because I didn't have it in me to give them much attention. All of my energy was focused on Danny, on being by his side for whatever was going to happen.

"You just sit there and sit there, and you wait. It's very hard to turn your mind off; it just keeps spinning. I literally felt like a dishrag, crying at any and all moments. People would call to check on him, and it put me into tears to explain what he was going through."

Some days Ron would go over to the hospital chapel and pray for a miracle. "I didn't make deals with God," he says. "I don't have a transactional relationship with Him—'If you do this, I promise I'll do that.' But I needed help and needed to talk, whether I was granted what I was praying for or not."

Ron's prayer *was* granted. After seven more days, Danny's blood flow had fully stabilized, and the doctors took him out of the induced coma. It seemed like things were holding.

But it turned out the entire ordeal needn't have happened. We learned that the aorta finally dissected as a reaction to years of astronomically high blood pressure that had been noted but never treated.

When blood courses through the arteries, it hits the artery walls; think of the way a gush of water comes through a rubber hose. If the pressure with which the blood snakes its way through is particularly intense—if the blood pressure is high—the walls of the "hose" suffer particular wear and tear. And if there's already an aneurysm—a weak spot in the artery that perhaps is already bulging out—that extra pressure is enough to tear the artery wall open, and the subsequent bleed can cause death to ensue almost immediately. The hope against hope continued to be that the third layer of Danny's artery wouldn't dissect.

We had known something wasn't right. Not only had Danny's voice been hoarse for two and a half years, it was getting quieter and quieter, to the point that he couldn't even sing, which he loved to do. We'd gone to seven different doctors to find out what was wrong, each one a different kind of specialist. They conducted ultrasounds, biopsied his vocal cords, and performed all kinds of other screenings. But they couldn't find anything wrong.

The one thing all the doctors did keep repeating was that Danny's blood pressure was astoundingly high—something like 210/160, when it should have been more like 120/80. But they didn't think that was the main issue. "When I would press them,"

Ron says, "the doctors would tell us, 'Well, the high blood pressure is secondary to what the real problem is. Once we get that figured out, the blood pressure will automatically go down.'" But it was the intense force of the high blood pressure that was burning up two layers of Danny's aorta. Things had finally come to a head.

Ron learned this once Danny's sisters signed the paper that said Ron could converse with the doctors. "I was explaining how Danny's voice had grown raspy," Ron says, "and the cardiologist asked, 'How long has that been going on?' When I told him, he explained that a lot of patients get voice box paralysis from high blood pressure, and that's what makes the voice weaker and weaker. It's a clue that the blood pressure needs to be brought down."

When all Danny's medical records were finally sent over to the hospital, they even had notations saying that Danny kept telling the doctors that his father and two of his sisters had high blood pressure; it ran in the family. He remembered that one nurse, after taking his blood pressure a year or two earlier, said, "Oh, I bet they're going to put you on blood-pressure-lowering medication." But they never did.

The cardiologist at the hospital told Ron that Danny's blood pressure was so high, his voice box never should have been biopsied. There was just too much risk in such a procedure.

At a certain point we talked about bringing suit. But although we discussed it extensively, we let it go. Danny did not want to go through the emotional stress that suing would have stirred up. He feared it would raise his blood pressure again. The two of us were angry, to be sure.

But as Danny put it, "Even if we win, it's not going to undissect my aorta." What we couldn't afford most of all was to let the anger eat at us, so we made a conscious decision to drop it and focus on ourselves, our lives.

Still, our tribulations were far from over. Soon after Danny was released from his coma, he started complaining that his back was hurting. "I felt as if I were lying on ballast stones," he says. "It was more than uncomfortable. It hurt."

Finally, after three days, a very good friend of ours from the horse circuit, Lisa Tolnitch, came to visit. She happens to be a breast cancer surgeon, but she was able to identify the problem almost immediately. When Danny told her that he felt as though he were lying on rocks, she rolled him over to have a look at his back. It turned out the inflatable bed he was on had a hole in it. He had been lying right on top of the coils; there were red circles on his back from where the springs were digging into him. It seemed to be one thing after another.

The doctors continued to monitor Danny after that. After a couple more weeks he was allowed out of bed to go to the bathroom. The doctors told us more than once that he was a walking miracle, like an oddity in a medical book having surpassed all odds.

At that point Danny was still fuzzy from all the drugs meant to keep him calm and quiet but was becoming more coherent. He said one day that he wanted new boxer shorts to wear in the hospital; he was tired of just wearing the hospital gown and constantly being exposed.

His sister Lynne was down from Wilmington, and she and Ron decided to go out for lunch rather than eat in the hospital cafeteria. On the way back they'd stop at the mall for the new underwear.

The hospital at that point was reconfiguring and repaving all the parking lots except for a very small one right by the hospital entrance. If you couldn't find a spot there, you'd have to drive down the road away from the building, and a shuttle bus would bring you back up. Ron didn't want to have to deal with that—they had already spent more time away from Danny on the shopping expedition than he felt comfortable with—so he suggested to Lynne when they got back that they wait at the small lot until someone pulled out rather than have to catch the shuttle and then wait for one to take them back to their cars late at night, when visiting hours were over.

Soon enough, they saw someone walking to her car, so Ron pulled over near the spot and put on his turn signal to let anyone else know that he'd be taking the space once the other driver pulled out. She took a while, but she finally backed away, and just as Ron was going to turn in, a tiny sports car sped around the corner and zipped into the space.

Normally, Ron would have just been annoyed but moved on. Something clicked in him, though. He got out of his car, tapped on the window, and told the young woman at the wheel that he had been waiting several minutes to pull into that space and had had his signal on the whole time.

"That's your fuckin' problem," the other driver responded.

"But I've been waiting."

"I don't care."

And with that she stepped out of her car, slammed the door, and walked casually toward the hospital entrance.

"I was on day fifteen or sixteen of spending twenty hours a day at the hospital," Ron says. "I felt like my head was going to explode, I was so angry at her. I told Lynne, 'You go to the room, and I'll drive down to the other parking lot and meet you up there.'"

Ron then put on the blinkers, turned off his car, took his key out of the ignition, and walked over to the woman's car. With the key still in his hand, he got on his knees and took the tire cap from the air valve of one of the tires, using the key to push the stem of the valve and flatten the tire to a pancake at the bottom. Then he calmly proceeded to the next tire—and the next. And the next.

"People were walking by and staring at me as the tires were going '*hssss*,'" Ron says. "I didn't care. My decorum, maybe my judgment, had snapped. I wasn't proud of myself. But with Danny finally doing better, I was able to exhale a little but couldn't take one more assault. I guess letting the air out of those tires was kind of a metaphor for the exhalation, and a message to the universe that at least *this* piece of being ignored wasn't going to go unanswered."

When Ron reached the room, Lynne said to him, "Ronnie, you've got a smirk on your face. What have you done?"

When he told her and Danny, the three of us laughed for several minutes—until Ron made true the old saying about laughing so hard he cried. "I guess it was kind of a catharsis," he says. "I was so relieved to have Danny awake and not getting worse that I was finally able to respond to all the terror, and maybe anger, that I was holding in."

But the real fallout from what had happened was only just beginning. Before Danny was released from the hospital, twenty-four days after he was admitted, the doctors sat Ron down and explained that Danny's life expectancy was in all likelihood going to be three years, maybe five if he was lucky. His aorta was like an already shredded hose with a bubble, or bulge, and the part that barely hung together was just waiting to rip apart. Even a slight rise in blood pressure, or something like the air bag going off in the car, could kill him in an instant. He would pop his aorta and bleed out.

He was going to have to go for CT scans several times a year, be on all kinds of blood-pressure medications for the rest of his short life.

In addition, he was never going to be allowed to ride a horse again. Even the best-trained rider falls off a horse sometimes; the horse bucks or rears. And if he fell off and hit his chest, it could be the end of him.

The doctors also told both of us that Danny was probably going to feel depressed. Danny recounts, "They said that after events like the one I had been through, it was almost guaranteed that I would become depressed. Even though you're feeling better, the memory of it comes back and the toll adds up."

But it wasn't just what Danny had been through medically. He had been riding horses since he was a little boy. He started out teaching himself. At a neighbor's, he would walk a horse away from the barn, then climb on, aim the horse back in the direction of the barn, and just start kicking to make the animal go. "It was mostly pine trees with some paths," he says, "and a lot of the paths went right under low branches. I couldn't steer around them because I didn't know how, so I would grab a branch and swing off. The horse would finish running back to the barn by itself.

"Later on, I thought it was so much fun that I would aim for a higher branch just so I could swing off onto it while letting the horse run ahead of me. Then I'd go get the horse again, lead it back out, and do it all over."

He wished for a horse for as long as he could remember—and

finally received that pony from his parents for Christmas when he was ten, winning the first of too many trophies to count.

"The event was pony jumping," he says. "The other kids had expensive ponies and jodhpurs and English saddles that fit, and there I was with my fifty-dollar horse in my little flannel shirt and jeans. But I took first place. Riding *was* me."

Of course, being a rider and trainer was what he had been doing professionally for decades. It wasn't like he had a desk job that he could quietly go back to. Not riding anymore was going to be a serious game changer.

We drove straight home to South Carolina from the hospital once Danny was released. Ron already had the dogs in the car. They were beyond thrilled to see Danny, and he to see them, but they knew something was different. Ron had jiggered the luggage so they would not be able to make their way to the front seat and climb on top of Danny. He was still too tender for that. It was hard for Danny. It was like not being able to hug your kids after not seeing them for a long time.

It was also confusing for the dogs, and they, with all the other dogs in our charge, were similarly confused when they were not allowed on the bed back at the house. Danny needed to remain very guarded with any movements made, and the smaller dogs had a habit of climbing on his chest while he was lying down, which for the time being was going to be out of the question. Even the little things were different now—dogs had slept in the bed with us for years.

Minnie, a dachshund/terrier mix, took it particularly hard. She was always so gentle and loving and didn't understand why her efforts to welcome Danny home with affectionate licks were being rebuffed. It hurt us not to be able to explain to Minnie why we were keeping her off the bed, but we truly had no choice.

Soon after we arrived back home after the ordeal, Ron called the one surgeon in the United States who at that time operated on dissected aortas to see if he could repair Danny's, someone out of Texas. But the doctor explained that the operation was pretty much available then only to people who needed repairs to the *ascending* aorta. An ascending aortic dissection is very easy to fix because it's only about two inches long; all the surgeon has to do is put an artificial sleeve over it to make more layers.

Danny's aneurysm was in his *descending* aorta, which is much longer and supplies blood to most of the body. And because his tear was so long, they'd have to take his abdominal organs out of his body, plus his heart (which meant putting him on a bypass machine), and would need to try to insert plastic tubing to replace the damaged part of his aorta that went to all of those organs and related tissue. The surgery would take twenty-eight to thirty hours. And the prognosis was a 30 percent chance of living through the surgery itself and, if he did, a 20 percent chance that he'd end up brain-dead because of the potential loss of blood during the operation. He could also end up paralyzed. The doctor recommended that we not even consider the surgery. "I would roll the dice and just try to live how you're living," the surgeon said.

So the aorta was never going to heal, and the depression set in as anticipated, exacerbated by the sudden lack of physical activity and loss of purpose. The instructions to Danny to take his own blood pressure several times a day and swallow all kinds of blood-pressure-managing medications only rendered things worse by making him feel like a perennial patient. He was not going to be able to free himself from the constant reminder that his life hung in the balance. Of course, we both felt like we were on a ticking time bomb.

"I was holding my breath every day," Ron says. "Any time Danny would tell me he didn't feel well—it could have just been indigestion or some little twinge—I would try not to act alarmed, but my heart would start pounding. 'Tell me exactly what you feel,' I would say. I would wonder, you know, is this . . . ? On a scale of one to ten, that fear, that knowledge about a life expectancy of three to five years, was a twenty. Every single moment it felt like the clock was ticking, and I would get scared if I saw him doing something, anything. I knew he didn't want to sit there and be a vegetable, but I was always worried about when even a small amount of activity would be too much."

For Danny himself, the foreboding went in a somewhat different direction. "It was not fear of dying or fear or pain," he says. "It was just very hard not doing what I did. It was a big blow to my identity. I hated being in places where people were riding and doing show courses. Sometimes the depression just engulfed me."

Ron understood this. "Danny was known throughout the country as a world-class hunter/jumper athlete," he says, "having won what you could consider the Triple Crown of hunter/jumper events all on the same horse—a feat no one else had ever accomplished. In 1989, shortly before the huge events we experienced that brought us into each other's lives, he came away with championships at the Pennsylvania National Horse Show, Washington International Horse Show, Madison Square Garden, Devon, and other shows throughout the country. He is also the winner of the Lifetime Achievement Award of the United States Hunter Jumper

Association. I knew that not being able to ride was going to be a kind of death of its own."

Danny found a way around the problem, however. He ignored the doctors' orders. This greatly alarmed Ron. He pleaded with Danny to please stop. "He didn't give me an ultimatum," Danny says. "He just told me it really scared him if I rode. But I couldn't not get back on a horse. It felt so wonderful. The only hard part was looking in everybody else's eyes—especially Ron's—and seeing the fear."

Danny finally did stop sometime later—when a horse he was in the midst of mounting one day reared straight up and then flipped over sideways. Danny, not wanting to get crushed under the stallion's fourteen hundred pounds, rolled off and backwards, out of the way, which was when a fence post jammed into his back and, from there, directly into his right lung, puncturing it. He also broke all his ribs in the accident. That locked down his diaphragm to the point that it couldn't expand and contract on the right side the way it was supposed to, blocking that lung from breathing in a full supply of oxygen.

He ended up in a hospital trauma unit for even longer than when his aorta dissected. And he lost his right lung during recuperation. It simply bled out.

Through the entire ordeal, during which the doctors used the same phrase for Danny as when his aorta dissected—"a walking miracle"—Ron once again had to deal with the fact that he was not Danny's spouse. "Even when Danny was conscious and said I could make decisions for him," he says, "the medical staff said no until I went and gathered the papers from our safe-deposit box. And even after I did, if a new doctor would come into the room, I'd have to explain and show my papers all over again."

In the wake of the accident, we really talked. This time, Danny knew that he must have received divine intervention with the remnants of his aorta remaining intact and understood that he truly could never ride again. Until he did.

"I was never anybody other than a rider," he says. "I mean, I always coached. I always taught. But the riding was who I was. Particularly with young horses, I felt like I was given a little bit of a gift to have a good rapport with them, to communicate with the ones that were barely broken and teach them without making them fear what they were learning. I loved doing that; I didn't want to leave it."

The riding went on for quite a while more, with Ron periodically protesting, knowing that it was to no avail. Then a riding mishap damaged the ribs on Danny's left side, where he still had a working lung. Breathing started to become difficult there, too.

That's when Danny talked to himself. "I really understood by that point how much Ron and others had been there for me, and why they all became incredibly tense every time I got on a horse. I knew that while I could play Russian roulette with my own life, it wasn't fair to spend my time on earth making everyone who loved me worry all the time. So I made a vow to *myself* that that was it and went out with a little bit of grace—maybe not with all the grace I would have liked to accumulate during my riding career but enough not to cause the man who loved me any more unnecessary anxiety.

"It was probably one of the toughest times in my life," Danny says. "I certainly had tougher times when I was losing my family members, but that's a different thing from when you know you have to lose a part of yourself. It's just very hard not doing what you do. I ended up seeing a psychiatrist for a while who helped me through the transition.

"I still train riders and horses, and I still judge competitions. That has become a big part of my work. But I had to come to terms with never being one with a horse again, with not personally ever being the one to compete. It's a passion I had to learn to let go of—some days better than others."

Of course, this change did not speak to the fact that time was not on our side whether Danny rode horses or not. As we approached the three-year mark, our anxiety skyrocketed. Says Danny, "I remember asking one of my doctors, 'So what should I be doing now? Getting my affairs in order?' I wasn't afraid of dying. I simply wanted to be ready. I just didn't want to go 'boomp' and be gone."

But the three-year mark came and went uneventfully. And so did the five-year mark, even though by that point we were still always talking about eventualities.

Around the eight-year mark we kind of stopped referring to it all the time. By that point the dogs had long been back to jumping into bed with us, snuggling with Danny as well as Ron and climbing on top of Danny when the mood struck.

We're now at about the fifteen-year mark—Gadget, Flo, Tillie, and Trifles have all long ago crossed the Rainbow Bridge—and we have learned not to make the dread a main focus of our lives. Becoming ever busier rescuing dogs has helped us escape from constant pondering. "I'd say I'm down from a twenty in terms of anxiety to about a ten," Ron says. "We don't talk about it so much anymore."

Still, not a day goes by that it doesn't cross our minds—several times. It is always there.

Chapter 6

Making It Official, Part 1

Angel was only about four years old but already completely blind. It was the saddest thing to see a young dog walking very slowly, not knowing what she might bump into and keeping away from the other dogs.

We had to keep a halo on the ten-pound fluff of Maltese and poodle—plastic tubing that arced out in a circle around her head so it would hit furniture and other objects before she did.

If we hadn't taken her in, the local shelter would have put her down. It wasn't only that no one seemed interested in adopting the little forlorn ball of curls. The shelter knew that even if Angel's blindness could be reversed, it would cost too much money. Most shelters have a limit on how much they will spend on a dog's medical needs before having to make a decision to put it down. And because Angel was no longer a puppy, even if she had her eyesight it wasn't clear that anyone would take her. People want puppies, or at least dogs that are only a year or two old.

We were up to about forty dogs by this point. Some were Katrina misfits who couldn't be adopted. Milly and Daisy, for instance, were still enjoying their eccentric lives. But there were now a number of others we picked up along the way—from shelters, from the side of the road, from wherever. The house was getting more worn still, and we had to remove the dining room table and push the chairs to the sides of the room in order to make way for more crates and dog beds. The dining table was actually the first piece of furniture to go, along with the sideboard and china cabinet. Gone were the days of our lavish dinner parties.

Fires in the kitchen fireplace became a thing of the past, too. That always used to be really nice at the end of a fall day—to build a fire in the kitchen and have dinner there. But the fireplace had become a spot to put doggie beds and blankets. The dogs loved to curl up in there—"Five, six, seven of them," Ron says. "They just loved that area. That was fine with us. We wanted them to feel relaxed, and in our mission, we were submitting to this gradual takeover. Our house was turning into their doghouse."

We knew there was no turning back after the success we had in the wake of Katrina. There was fulfillment in rescuing beings who had no recourse, many of whom had been abandoned by their human families. But it was more than fulfillment. Taking care of forsaken animals simply became more and more of who we were. And we never said no to medical care, no matter how costly. It was as though, after Katrina, we were drawn into the ever-whirling storm of abandoned pets, going as fast as we could to fill in gaps to tend to them.

We contacted a veterinary ophthalmologist two and a half hours away in Charleston, not knowing if Angel's blindness was reversible but wanting to find out. Was it glaucoma? Diabetes? Was she born that way?

It turned out the reason for her milky white eyes and attendant lack of sight was juvenile cataracts. The doctor gave no guarantees but thought he had a good chance of being able to restore her vision, or at least most of it. The two surgeries would set us back more than $11,000—a little more than $5,500 for each eye.

Ron looked over our finances. We were going to have to take out more money from our retirement account, with yet another stiff pre-withdrawal tax penalty. The retirement nest egg continued to dwindle, and it made him nervous; he is the one who takes care of all our financial issues. But he made the call to our investment broker. "It was never a question of whether we would do it," Ron says, "just a matter of deciding whether to dig deeper into a home equity loan or our retirement savings."

During the day or so that it took for the transaction to go through, we happened to receive a call. It came out of the blue from a lawyer up in Michigan named Danielle McCluskey who had learned of our efforts.

"I had actually met Danny many years earlier," Danielle says. "He showed my mare at a horse show in Kentucky.

"He didn't remember me, and I wasn't calling about horses, anyway. I had seen Danny and Ron working to adopt out dogs one time at Blowing Rock," a charity horse show in North Carolina that raises money for education and other charitable causes such as a local fire department. "I hadn't thought much about it other than that I'm all for humane treatment of animals," Danielle says. "But then my friend Beth Graves moved from Michigan to Wellington, Florida. And Beth and a photographer got together to create a calendar for the guys that was meant to be used as a fundraiser to help them in their dog-rescue efforts.

"They were bouncing around other ideas for raising money when Beth asked them if they were a 501(c)3—a nonprofit organization. They weren't. That meant they couldn't claim any of the money they spent on dogs as a tax deduction, and it also meant that anyone who donated money to their cause couldn't deduct the contribution on their own tax returns. In fact, some people they knew had wanted to make sizable donations to their rescue effort but pulled back when they found out the donations wouldn't be tax-deductible.

"Beth texted me," Danielle recounts: "'I gave Ron Danta your phone number. He and Danny R are not a 501(c)3. You HAVE to do this.'"

When Ron and Danielle first talked he apologized for not remembering her. "No, I met Danny *years* ago," she assured him. She also told him she knew of his and Danny's efforts during Katrina. Then they talked dogs.

"The minute you start speaking with Ron or Danny," Danielle says, "the passion and the love that they have for all these different strays come through in every word. I was so motivated. My heart was touched, and I just wanted to help them in whatever way I could. Dogs that people would be counting out—that a shelter could not afford to take care of and that no one would adopt—*those* were they dogs they were interested in. They helped those dogs not just medically but also by training them and showing them how to be loving animals so they could find a great home for them. Their hearts were *huge*. So many of the dogs they had taken on were special needs.

"I knew the only way to keep the mission moving forward was to fundraise, but they were doing it all out of pocket, and that's where the lawyer part of me kicked in. 'You've got to do this in a way that protects you,' I said. 'You're engaging in charitable efforts, but you're trying to do it all independently. Let's utilize the great resources of the law, which permits you to start a nonprofit. It will allow people who want to be charitable to give money to a great cause. And it will save you money on your own taxes. You'll be able to accomplish even more going forward.'"

Danielle's thinking caught Ron off guard, and Danny, too, when Ron explained it to him. "We weren't considering the future," Danny says. "We were too busy to have any foresight. We just did what we did. Also, we didn't think we had a facility to qualify. We just had the house—and my farm for some of the bigger dogs. There was no established kennel. The government would think, 'Oh, these boys are just trying to get some money by keeping dogs in their house.'"

Danielle told us that wouldn't be a problem. And we sure could have benefited from donations. Up until that point, we had a couple of people who would send $5 a month. "We actually put our hands on it," Danny says. "We would open the mail and say, 'Look at that. Mrs. So-and-So sent another check.' We'd call the person to thank them personally or send back a handwritten note."

The thought of easing our financial burden was enticing. But when Danielle told us that our rescue would have to have a board that met every so often, a big blinking CAUTION sign went up in our heads. "Oh, great," Danny remembers feeling. "The board is going to say we can't do things the way we always have, which is to spend as much as necessary to make a dog better. They're going to say we can only spend so much per animal. What we have been doing from our hearts is now going to be done according to a business model, with no effort to save every dog and hold on to it as long as necessary, even forever if need be."

"Most shelters do have limits," Ron says. "If you have to spend more than a certain amount to help a dog, it has to be euthanized. But we believed that once we took on a dog, that dog was part of our family. We would spend more than $10,000 on a single operation if that's what was required—and sometimes did, as was about to happen with Angel. How could we not?"

Adds Danny, "We were very nervous that a board would overturn that approach, blocking us from letting a dog live its best life. A board's thinking might have prevented us from taking on Angel, and she would have been euthanized."

But Danielle assured us that she would protect our efforts as the founders and that we would be able to run the operation the way we had always seen fit. She would include a provision that a dog's outcome would always remain in our hands. She would put it in the by-laws. And she would do all the paperwork *pro bono*.

How could we refuse? At the very least we thought that becoming a bona fide nonprofit might enable us to hire more people to help out. At that point we had just Karen Odom working at the house. It was only the three of us, so when we had to go off to a horse show to earn our keep, we would overload Karen with all those dogs. It really was more than one person could handle, although she would bring friends to assist in our absence.

And there really were a lot of expenses. So many of the abandoned dogs we took in needed to be spayed or neutered. We had a kind of tunnel vision about it, never adding up what we were spending. We couldn't afford to look. It would throw us off track from trying to save all the dogs, trying to figure out who would adopt them, trying to make it all work. We were always going as fast as we could.

We had heard about how many nonprofits struggle to attract donors, but at the same time felt excited. Maybe, we thought, some of our friends in the horse business would send us twenty dollars here, forty dollars there. Anything would help, especially since unlike other rescue operations we never charged an adoption fee of several hundred dollars to recoup some of the up-front wellness costs. We were just happy if someone wanted to take a dog and love it for the rest of its life. So we said yes, not really knowing what we were in for.

Danielle had a thousand questions for us in order to be able to fill out the papers. Also, having always been just a pop-and-pop operation, we had to learn from the ground up about keeping receipts for everything; documenting everything we did; putting a system in place to make sure that money earmarked for a specific purpose by a contributor went to that purpose and nothing else. We didn't even have a name for the new rescue. Everybody in the horse world who had ever adopted from us would just say they had a Danny-and-Ron dog.

We struggled to quickly come up with a name because Danielle didn't want to delay filing the documentation with the federal government. Paws and Claws, Pooch Palace, Dog Retrievers, Fetch-A-Pet—we brainstormed all kinds of cutesy monikers, but each fell flat, not really reflecting our mission in any meaningful way. Goading us along, Danielle and a friend of ours in the horse world named Nardeen Henderson encouraged us to just go with Danny & Ron's Rescue. "Keep it simple," they advised.

So we did. And Danielle sent in the paperwork. In the meantime, the money for Angel's eye operations had been transferred from our retirement account to our bank account. We ordered the surgeries, steadfast in our decision but still dreading the possibility that she would not gain her sight and that the funds would have been spent for naught.

The doctor thought things went successfully, but it was going to take a little bit to learn to just what degree Angel's vision would be restored. She had to stay in the hospital for two days afterward, and then she was sent home with a variety of eye drops. One had to be given every hour; one, every two hours. We wondered when the outcome would be clear.

We didn't have to wonder long. The minute Angel walked into the kitchen she moved her paws about as if she were dancing. She was discovering the world she had known only by scent and hearing, and she was *so* excited. She immediately started running around the room, tossing toys in the air and playing with the other dogs. Our sad, withdrawn girl had become a fluffy wind-up toy. We cannot explain in words the joy such a transformation brings. We had seen none of that kind of activity before, absolutely none. She would just sit still, waiting for something to happen to her.

It was going to take a while before we could adopt her out to a loving family. We wanted to be the ones to finish giving her the eye drops, and we wanted to be able to do a recheck with the ophthalmologist and make sure everything was healing correctly. We couldn't let her go to a new home on the chance that something might go south and her new family would want to return her, traumatizing her once again.

We were happy to have more time with her, to be able to enjoy her in her new state. What a pleasure to have her jump up on the bed to snuggle with us, then run around the mattress excitedly as if to say to the other dogs, "Isn't this great! What a wonderful life we're living!"

Angel's was the last surgery we paid for before Danny & Ron's Rescue officially became a nonprofit organization. Maybe the next time we had to order an expensive operation to change a dog's life, we would have help.

But first, we had to hold our kickoff board meeting. We had no idea what a board actually did. We were not from the corporate world and had always conducted our lives by the seat of our pants. But, dutifully, we pulled a meeting together. Having regular board meetings was a requirement of the articles of incorporation.

Ron served as president and Danny as vice president. Our other board members were Ron's sister, Diane, Danny's sister Lynne, and Danielle. And Danielle was as "in" as a sister could be, and not just because she did all the paperwork for free. She had already adopted Sparty—a little black geriatric pug that we had found running down the middle of the road, covered in fleas. When we first touched him, his skin literally moved because there were so many fleas on it; they had made him nearly bald, and he was also severely anemic because of all the blood loss from their bites.

Sparty, like Angel, was blind, but there was no fixing it. Fortunately, his disability didn't make him sad and withdrawn, the way Angel's had.

"We called him recklessly blind," Danielle says. "He thought he could do *anything*. He'd play blind dog fetch, working a room from corner to corner until he found what you had tossed for him to retrieve. Then he'd wag his tail as happily as possible and bring the toy back to you to toss again. He was a sweet, loving dog from the day we brought him home, even though he had been through so much."

With Danielle and our own sisters as our fellow board members, we knew we were in good hands. At our first gathering we basically went over what we already all knew: If you're a dog who becomes part of Danny & Ron's Rescue, you will never have to worry again. You will never be put in a shelter or back on the street, and you will never be euthanized because of a lack of money. You will be microchipped with our phone number in case you ever get lost. And if someone who adopts you from us ever decides they can't or don't want to take care of you anymore, even after ten years, they have to return you to us rather than decide on their own what is the best course of action for you or who you should live with. We will send transportation if they can't provide it. We even developed a form that adopters had to sign showing that they agreed to all this before they were allowed to take a dog from our home.

Then we went about our business as usual, working horse shows and taking care of the dogs. We figured donations would start to roll in. It was just a matter of time.

One day during this interval we drove to Lowe's to pick up some fencing material for Danny's farm. Ron had already gotten in line to pay when Danny wandered off to the store's garden center, coming back with what looked for all the world like a dead orchid.

"Another dead brown thing in a pot?" Ron asked drolly.

"Danny has a penchant for picking up half-dead plants that belong in the garbage," he explains.

"It's eighty percent off," Danny replied. Ron rolled his eyes, and off to the car with the fencing went the drooping, flowerless orchid. When we arrived home, Danny placed it in a sunny spot by the kitchen window.

Over the course of a couple of months or more, he dutifully watched over it, turning it this way and that toward or out of the sun, watering it, and adding nutrients to the soil. Nothing came of it. Nor did anything come of our having officially turned into a nonprofit. Not a single donation trickled in.

Finally, our friend Nardeen suggested that we needed a website. We had absolutely zero experience with that sort of thing. A lot of people didn't. It was 2008, and while social media was gearing up, it was not yet the way of life it is now. We didn't have a website for our horse-training business, either—it was all word of mouth. We didn't even *go* to websites. Our purchases were all brick-and-mortar. The idea of building our own website was particularly daunting. We are far from computer geeks.

But we bought a "Build Your Own Website" disk, and Nardeen put together the site for us—DannyRonsRescue.org—then taught Ron how to put up pictures of dogs with their stories. She even taught Ron how to put the word "ADOPTED" in large letters across a dog's profile once it had gone to a loving home.

On top of that, some of the more prestigious equine magazines published articles about our "new" dog rescue and included the website's URL in them. And Danielle instructed us to get business cards, which was a big to-do with all of us putting our heads together about how to design them. With the website, the magazine articles, and handing out the cards at horse shows, we figured, *now* the money would start rolling in.

But it didn't. It all seemed like a lot of window dressing that had been for naught. To tell you the truth, we kind of forgot about it. There was always so much going on, not the least of which was Angel's going to her forever home.

Once we finished her course of eye drops and the doctor determined that she had healed without complications, we began to put out the word that she was up for adoption. We didn't think to use the new website. That's how unfamiliar we were with going online to do anything.

Because Angel was white and fluffy, there was quite a bit of local interest in her even though she was no longer a puppy. But one lovely woman named Evelyn turned out to be the obvious match. She drove a couple of hours from North Carolina to the doghouse and fell instantly in love with her—and Angel with Evelyn. That in itself didn't distinguish Evelyn in any particular way. Now that Angel had her sight and delighted in everyone, dogs and people alike, folks tended to fall in love with her, which only served to reinforce her affectionate nature.

But chatting with Evelyn on the kitchen floor, where Angel had jumped into her lap and was giving her kisses as she wiggled happily, we learned that she, too, had gone sightless after experiencing a torn retina resulting from an eye injury that the doctors doubted could be reattached. But against the odds, she also returned to full sight. With tears streaming down Evelyn's cheeks as she told her story, and then with our own eyes brimming, how could her home not be the right one for Angel to go off to?

As everyone knows, in this world many things happen for which we never see reasons, but the reasons are there even if we can't divine them. This time, the reason was unmistakable.

Ron had to leave the house before Evelyn put Angel in the car. That's how it often goes. We cry when we take a dog in because it has often been through more than any living being should have to bear, and then one or both of us becomes particularly bonded, and we go off and cry when the dog leaves. It's not that we fear we've made the wrong decision. We know that every dog deserves his or her own home and should not have to share the love and devotion with dozens of others—a fact of life that is unavoidable in our house. But having to let go of a dog we have come to love often still proves heartbreaking, no matter how beautifully it is matched with its new person.

At the same time, the cycle is what keeps us going through the hard times of rescue—the times that we find dogs so terribly abused or neglected. The hope that a happy moment will come for that dog if he begins to receive all the love and devotion he's entitled to heals our wounds even as we know a new wound will form again when the next rescued animal leaves. It's a constant scabbing over.

We heard from Evelyn soon after she arrived home with Angel (and many times after that) how grateful she was to have the little dog in her life, adding to our security in having done the right thing.

It wasn't long after Angel found her forever home that Danny's beloved mare Gracie foaled. She had been pregnant through the ordeal with Angel.

The baby horse, a rose-gray colt, wasn't ready at first to venture out into the pasture late at night with the other mares and foals, and as a doting "Dad," Danny would drive over to keep him and his mother company. "I loved that mare," Danny says, "and would go to feed her carrots and other treats when she wasn't nursing, stroke her neck, and also put down some more bedding. I'd muck the stall, too."

Ron would sometimes go over with him—the breeding farm was two houses down—but one evening it was unseasonably hot, especially right in the stall, and Ron was in a hurry to leave, anyway, because he had dinner on the stove. Danny told him he'd be back home in a few minutes; he just wanted to change Gracie's water buckets.

As Ron left, he absentmindedly pulled the stall door shut and made sure the latch was in place. "You never want to leave the door cracked where the foal can shoot out," he says.

But that meant Danny had no way to get out when he was ready to leave a short time later. "It was stifling in there," he says, "and I have allergies, which only made things worse. And the sliding doors and the windows were so heavily mesh-wired that I couldn't even get a finger through to try to open something or get the lock unlatched. I tried calling Ron on the cell phone, but there was no reception in the barn. It was built too tightly.

"So I started doing what anybody else might do—scream at the top of my lungs. For two hours. During that time I thought I might be able to get out through the attic. There was a vent in the ceiling, and Gracie let me climb on her back and then stand up straight to see if I could shimmy through. It was like a scene out of *The Shawshank Redemption* except with no actual escape. I couldn't reach where I needed.

"Finally, I took off my belt and squeezed it through the slight crack of the locked stall door. My aim was to hook the buckle onto the door handle. That didn't work, either."

Eventually, Ron came back to get Danny. "What the hell are you still doing here?" he said, annoyed, not realizing what had happened. "I thought you were coming in a few minutes. Dinner has been ready for more than an hour."

Danny, of course, had his own reason to be angry, and the two of us arrived back at the house hungry and out of sorts. As Ron reheated the meal in the microwave and readied the dinner plates, Danny thumbed through the pile of mail on the kitchen island, a daily collection made thick by bills and catalogues. By that point we had removed the kitchen table to make room for more dogs and had begun taking all our meals on stools at the island, often with interested housemates hanging on our every move to see if we might offer anything up.

"Ron!" Danny called out suddenly.

"What?" Ron responded gruffly. He thought we were still fighting.

Danny didn't answer. Ron looked up to find him holding a hundred-dollar check. Someone had sent in the first tax-deductible donation to Danny & Ron's Rescue. The website worked! Money was going to start coming in, and we were going to be able to save more dogs than ever!

We went to bed happy that night, ten or twelve dogs piling in with us, and our spirits were buoyed even more when we awoke the next morning. A brilliant violet-colored orchid had bloomed on Danny's plant.

Danielle McCluskey is the lawyer who turned our rescue efforts into an official nonprofit enterprise—without charging us a penny. Here she is with hound mix Autumn, one of at least half a dozen Danny & Ron dogs she has adopted over the years. Autumn was originally found on the side of the road and lived in two other homes before she came to stay permanently with Danielle and her husband, Dean.

Chapter 7

Blanket Hour

S̶shhhh. It's Blanket Hour.

    On afternoons that we have some extra time, we—or the staff we were able to start hiring once donations began coming in—will spread out some blankets on the kitchen floor and quietly sit there in case some of the more scared animals would like to approach. We can't do it every day. If we're not making four or five visits to different veterinary clinics for help with various dogs' medical problems, we're often driving to shelters that might be as far as a couple of hours away in order to rescue dogs about to be euthanized. But when we are able, it can prove wonderfully therapeutic for the dogs who are particularly anxious.

The kitchen is one of many rooms in the house devoted to

different dogs who have different needs at different times—a system we developed as we went along. For instance, we turned the screened-in porch behind the dining room into a four-season room where those dogs who have communicable illnesses or other serious medical issues are quarantined. Called the Q-room by us and staff, it's a good space for them because it's not a high-traffic area. We used to have a hot tub for ourselves there, but we removed it and had a sink installed instead for washing wounds during bandage changing and also for cleaning equipment.

The front bedroom is reserved almost strictly for litters of puppies. People will often abandon pregnant dogs (that they ne-glected to spay but then let outside on their own), and we fre-quently have two litters at a time. It can work out very well. One time, one of two new mothers that were "rooming" together with their pups was not able to produce any milk, and the other mother stepped in as wet nurse. All the tiny dogs from both litters thrived. (If we become really jammed for space for new puppy litters, we use the shower stall in our bathroom. We don't mind having given it up and showering in the hall bathroom; it's a safe place for newborns.)

On the other side of the house, next to the garage, the laundry room serves as a kind of rehab facility—a place where dogs recu-perate from major surgery. A quiet zone, it's away from the may-hem of the rest of the place, and convalescing dogs are not enticed to play and break stitches or otherwise become too active when they should be resting. We also like to think that they might feel relaxed, lulled, by the hum of the commercial washer and dryer we keep in the garage. With nineteen loads a day—including dog beds from all over the house as well as crate pads and towels from when some of the animals have accidents (and that says nothing

of the nine hundred wee wee pads we go through each week)—
the two machines are constantly whirring.

As for the living room, it tends to be claimed by the larger
dogs. We also have some bigger, particularly energetic dogs at the
farm—border collies and other working dogs who need plenty of
exercise for their emotional well-being. They can run around the
twenty-two acres there without our having to be afraid that they
will dig out and run away; we installed concrete along the entire
perimeter going down three and a half feet into the earth. They
can't jump over the fencing, either. We put in a hot wire at the top
of all the perimeter fencing to keep in the climbers.

Keeping escapees safe is critical. We have two Great Pyrenees,
Oscar and Molly, who will live out their lives at the farm because
they could not remain secure at people's homes. They had first
lived with a woman in Georgia who finally had to surrender them
because they kept making their way out to the highway, and she
was afraid they'd be hit by a car. We then adopted them out to
a Massachusetts couple with a lot of land for them to enjoy, but
they kept doing their Houdini thing there, too. These days they
hang out with the other larger dogs and, like a number of the
Katrina dogs so many years ago, they like watching the farrier do
his work on the horses' feet. If they could talk you'd hear them
telling the farrier, "You need to file down that hoof a little more"
or "Nice job on the shoeing."

The bigger dogs at the house are content to stay put—they
often have energy to burn, but not too much of it—and they have
a doggie door in the living room that lets them go outside at will.
They have the complete run of that room, climbing onto couches
or chairs or wherever else they want to lounge. They frequently
enjoy coming in from outside and then passing from the living

room to our bedroom to mingle and get a comforting pat or stroking behind the ears if one of us is sitting at the computer doing paperwork for the rescue or for our equine clients.

The kitchen has a doggie door, too. It's where the little dogs tend to spend their days, and that's one of the reasons we have Blanket Hour in there. For dogs who have been through a lot, smaller dogs might prove a little less scary. And that's the whole point of Blanket Hour—to help newly arrived dogs who are scared because of the abuse they have been through learn that they are safe now and that the world does not have to be a frightening, harmful place.

It works best from late fall through winter and on into early spring. When the weather is warm and sunny, someone is outside with the dogs much of the time—throwing balls, playing with them in the doggie swimming pool, helping them balance on the teeter-totter and the climbing ladder. The new, timid dogs can watch from the sidelines, see how much fun the other, confident dogs are having, and make decisions on whether to join in. Many spend a lot of time over in a corner or in the gazebo, broadening their trust from afar. They can even go back inside through the doggie door if all the activity proves to be too much commotion for them—whatever they want, as long as they know they can do what they need to feel comfortable.

But when the weather is cold and brisk, it just kind of feels right to hunker down and spend time together inside. The way Blanket Hour works is that either one of us or a member or two of the staff will set out a big blanket in front of the kitchen fireplace and sit on it. What happens next is that some of the outgoing dogs—those who have lived with us for a while or who came to us with resilient personalities no matter what they have been through—wiggle-waggle on over and climb onto our laps and start kissing us. A few of them actually become very excited when we unfold the blanket, wagging their tails and even approaching eagerly from other rooms. They know the routine and understand that in a very busy household, it's time for attention just for them.

The timid ones, often but not always newly arrived, watch from what they consider a distance—perhaps under a table or in a corner. That's frequently the case with puppy mill dogs. They come from some of the roughest situations, never having been let out of a cage their entire lives, never having known tenderness but kept solely as a supply stock just for breeding and sales. After a while, a shy one might come a little closer and glance in our direction. Sitting on the floor, you're no longer high above a dog, and that might make a fearful dog feel a little more confident about interacting. At the same time, perhaps one of the dogs on the blanket will reach out and start playing with him a little bit.

Because the kitchen is kind of a landing strip for people coming into the house as well as for going from one part of the house to another, there is always movement. The staff is talking, taking crate pads out to the wash, taking dogs to the tub by the laundry room to have a bath, going out to the yard to pick up poop.

That might sound counterintuitive—to have frightened dogs where people are constantly going to and fro. But it's a gentle way to help them learn that people can be safe, that people can protect and take care of them. We try to keep things very quiet; everybody goes about their business with the volume down. They also don't look at the dogs or walk toward them unless they get a sense that perhaps one of them might accept a little seemingly absentminded stroking along the muzzle or ears as they walk by. They keep their eyes up, even if they reach down to pet while they are moving along. In the dog world, a direct gaze can be interpreted as very confrontational, aggressive. So can being approached straight on. Dogs will often follow a banana-shaped arc to reach another dog as a way of letting it know that it doesn't mean any trouble. Dogs are lovers, not fighters, unless they feel they have no choice, and they have all kinds of body language to indicate that they mean no harm. We apply their body language when they are feeling threatened so they know we respect them and are not looking to harm them. We play by *their* Marquess of Queensbury rules.

We never have any particular frightened dogs in mind when we do Blanket Hour, nor do we ever try to coax any dog toward us. That's important with rescue dogs in general. Most of them have been chased—either by their original owners to be harmed or perhaps by good Samaritans to be taken to a shelter. And then they are touched against their will to get an injection or other medical care. All the activity has been *toward* them, and it makes them feel like they have no agency in their own lives, so it's very important that they come to you on their own terms (like Simba did, when we found him at the side of the road while listening to that *Lion King* tape). Otherwise, you're invading their trust. You can't force a sense of security; you have to allow them to be able to tell you the point at which they feel secure.

"If you just plop down on the floor and want a certain dog to come to you," Danny says, "it's not going to happen. It has to be their idea. They have an innate instinct for when something is about them, and if they're trepidatious to begin with, they won't feel comfortable about having attention aimed their way. But if you have a little time, not five minutes but longer, and they get to watch what other dogs do and observe how they respond to being gently cooed over and see you're not after them, that it's just let-go time, they learn to want to be a part of it."

It can take five days, or it can take five months, or a year or two. Cotton was one of those who took a very long time. A little white poodle mix, he was a stray who had been hanging out at a woman's house and started pooping on her porch. She didn't want him there to begin with—he never was allowed inside the house—and to deal with the mess, she put a diaper on him. But she wouldn't change it. It was filled with his feces, which was filled with worms. There was so much excrement he essentially stopped defecating by trying to hold it in, and his bowels became backed up.

Her kids loved him, but she said she "didn't want the dog shittin' on her porch anymore," and someone we knew who lived near her got wind of the situation, so he ended up in our care. Not only did he have impacted stools—once he ignored the urge he stopped being able to "go"—but he was also extremely skinny and lethargic. On top of rarely, if ever, being fed, he was really being overtaken by the worms.

The vet estimated that he was one or two years old, barely having reached adulthood and having known nothing but abuse and deprivation throughout his entire life to that point. The doctor started treatment by shaving his behind and giving him laxatives. He also began a deworming process that took almost two years to completely resolve. Every time he went in for a checkup, and, we hoped, would receive an "all clear," he'd still have the worms—or had developed another kind. Throughout the ordeal he was nothing but bones.

He had to stay at the vet's for a couple of weeks before we

were able to bring him home because he needed an IV line for fluids and various medicines. When we did bring him back to the house, he was scared to death. If you so much as walked in his direction he would bolt. He was never aggressive—just extremely insecure and avoidant. He wanted to isolate himself and keep away from people. He had obviously had some bad experiences at the hands of human beings besides the lady with the porch.

"In the beginning, his whole body would shake with fear," Ron says. "He would quake so much it was like a person with the DTs going through withdrawal. It hurt us that we couldn't pick him up and cuddle him.

"It's heartbreaking, really. Your heart says to scoop them into your arms, but your intellect reminds you, no. I always think, who did what to this dog—to make this dog so fearful and insecure about a human being? On so many levels it just rips your heart out wondering how anybody could abuse an animal to make it reach this point."

Says Danny, "We did have to pick him up every day because we had to follow him around the yard to get him back into the house or place him in his crate to give him his special food while he was healing. He was too scared to come when we called him. We would try to hold him to make it nice, but he was so stiff and concerned that we did it for as little time as possible. It makes you terribly sad—and angry for what brought the dog to this place that you don't even know about—not to be able to follow your instinct and hold them close to you."

"We get so hurt and angry and embarrassed and disappointed in humanity—that humans could act this way," Ron adds. "But people abuse children and wives and everything else. These poor animals become victims, just like the rest of the victimized."

"And you know it's abuse even though you weren't there to witness it," Danny says. "A neglected dog will continue to love no matter what. Neglect is something a dog would never blame you for. They don't know any better. With abuse, it's instinctual. They turn into fearful biters—or, as in Cotton's case, they run. There are consequences."

It was clear that Cotton had never been in a house before. He was so unused to everything, and he felt overwhelmed. He would watch the other dogs go through the doggie door to do their business and frolic, and at first he declined to go with them. He was too afraid to make a move. So he eliminated inside, and that was okay. We knew the problem was fear and that he couldn't be rushed through his emotions.

As we anticipated, he did come to realize soon enough that he could follow the other dogs out and relieve himself. (Poop is always picked up right away, so we were not concerned that the other dogs would get worms.) But he kept to himself in the yard and was so fearful of people that he wouldn't come back in. He would remain outside all day and evening, and it would take at least four people to herd him back into the house come nighttime. That was always one of the times that somebody would have to hold him, even though we knew it wasn't good for him at that point.

During Blanket Hour, he started out remaining at the far end of the kitchen and just watching, taking the long view, as Ron puts it. Over time, he began to slowly edge his way closer and closer. He then reached the point at which he would get onto the blanket and immediately back up, then come onto the blanket again only to instantly back up again. That cha-cha became almost like a little game—and we never coaxed him at any point;

it all had to be his decision. As he advanced, he came closer and closer to whoever was on the blanket and finally would even get next to the person.

He started out coming onto the blanket from behind, as tends to happen with the scared dogs. They feel better if they can see you but you can't see them. They run into the now-unused fireplace at our backs and then one day slowly creep forward and sniff your neck. It can become a little complicated at times because we have a little Chihuahua/Boston terrier mix named Amelia, a cream-colored button of a thing with a pale butterscotch stripe along her back, and she has decided she *owns* the fireplace. Quite a quirky little event in herself—small and charming but also feisty and bossy (she sometimes goes through the doggie door like a wheelbarrow, standing only on her front legs with her hind legs straight up in the air)—she claimed a bed in the fireplace as her throne a long time ago. Fortunately, the self-proclaimed queen (who is relentless when she decides it is time for you to pick her up and cuddle her) allows certain other dogs to have their doggie beds in there with her, and we also spread out a couple of beds on the floor in front of the hearth as well. The area is kind of like a lodge, but only for "members." It is truly amazing the way dogs work things out for themselves.

Cotton and Amelia get along—they love each other and like to sleep side by side sometimes, in fact. And Amelia has always allowed him into her throne room *as long as she isn't eating.* (Heaven help you if you get near her food bowl while a meal is in progress.) Which is why he was always allowed to approach us from inside the fireplace pretty much at will. And one day, after doing his little two-step for months and months, he turned the proverbial corner and jumped onto Danny's lap. It was a huge victory for Cotton—and for us—that he was able to break through the fear like that. You can only imagine how difficult it is to remain quiet and calm when you want to give a dog tons of praise for his bravery and make a big to-do of it. Danny settled for gentle stroking, but we can't describe the emotional satisfaction that comes with knowing a dog has finally learned—at least to some degree—that people won't hurt him ever again. We know it from the moment a dog comes into our lives, but the best part is the moment that the dog knows it.

We think of it as the bridge over troubled waters that the dog has to cross. We and our staff are the bridge, and we can't push a dog to cross it. He has to be allowed to decide on his own to walk over, and at his own pace.

But even when a dog first makes the crossing, it's not that everything changes in that instant. It took about two and a half years after that first foray onto Danny's lap for Cotton to trust anyone other than the two of us or Karen—our very first staff member. When anyone else so much as came near him, he would back up. He wouldn't dart away, but he definitely was carving out his own, separate space.

Gradually, however, he continued to come around. Over time, he began to kind of prance and dance on the blanket. It was his body's way of expressing his feeling of security.

Then, a long while later, he began following dogs into the bedroom at night. He would not come onto the bed. He slept on a doggie bed that we set out just for him. But he was content there—until he finally decided to climb up the doggie stairs we put beside the bed to make it easier for him to come up if he wanted to.

He soon experimented with diving under the covers. He could

feel very safe there being near us but not having to have us look at him. He will still often sleep under the covers even if the sheets are tight on the bed, but he has also learned to love sleeping on top of our heads, too, almost like a hat. But that took a *loooong* time.

And even today, he doesn't quite handle things the way the other dogs do. Many of the dogs have their own crates, and they get fed in them and often like to sleep in them. An unlocked crate is like a cozy man cave or she shed to a dog, not a prison. And it helps us because every morning we feed all the dogs in the house ourselves before the staff arrives and we go off to train horses for a few hours until we come back and make the rounds for vet appointments and shelter visits. The reason the crates make our work easier is that they allow us to give different diets depending on the animals' medical needs. Some have heart disease and require a low-sodium diet. Others have kidney failure and need diets with less phosphorus to slow the progression of their illness. Others still might need a relatively low-fat diet because they are prone to bouts of pancreatitis. The crates keep the dogs from digging into one another's food. We also dispense medications in the crates, managing to keep the dogs separate until they consume everything meant just for them and no other animal.

Each dog becomes very accustomed to the crate he or she goes to. Some even prefer a second-story crate—a crate on top of a crate. The comfort their crates give them is so strong that when it's time for lights-out at 9 p.m. and we shake the treat jar, a number of the dogs who like to nestle in their "dens" for the night go running to their individual ones. Even some of the new dogs get it so quickly that it looks like a piece of choreography as they all dash to their separate spots.

But not Cotton. He has his own trademark bedtime snack routine. As all the other dogs excitedly make their way to their crates, he will climb onto the bed and prance and dance—Danny calls it the Cotton Dance—and we have to play a little game with him where you just keep leaning in until you can grab him, put him in his crate, and watch him eat his food. Now about twelve years old, he still does that every single evening and clearly enjoys the routine.

Cotton has come such a long way since he entered our lives almost a dozen years ago. An old man now, what started out as his in-treatment center for emotional healing has become his comfortable old-age home. Our aim is always to place a rehabilitated dog in a new home so he can have a forever life without having to share the love with a hundred other animals, even though it's hard to say goodbye to a dog who's ready to be loved by another household—always. But when someone, or some family, goes crazy over their new pet and tags us in picture after picture on Facebook—"Here's So-and-So cuddled on the couch with me"; "Here's So-and-So enjoying a lick of ice cream"—that means everything to us. It's so gratifying to know we've taken a dog from Death Row, from some unimaginable situation, and helped it to finally have a good life. We also love that the love is paid forward because it saves so many *people.* It is difficult to describe how restored people feel when they take home a dog who was missing from their lives. So many adopters say to us, "I don't know what I'd do without this dog." It's a refrain we hear over and over.

But that could never have been Cotton's fate. He will always be one of our sanctuary dogs who lives out his life here at the doghouse. It took him a good five or six years to reach the point that he became as secure as he was ever going to get, but he's still a nervous sort. And to have pulled the carpet out from under him and make him adjust to yet another situation would simply have been cruel. "We love him so much and just couldn't ever be the reason he was let down again," says Danny.

We don't even take him anywhere. He doesn't travel with us to horse expos like some of the other dogs do because we don't want to confuse him and raise the specter of apprehension ever again. "Taking him out of the one place that he has come to believe in would prove traumatizing," Ron comments.

But he has learned that it's okay to trust people other than us and Karen. He's not what you would call an extrovert, but he loses his anxiety about almost every staff member in the house once they've been there awhile. He still has little twinges, but his fear level has really diminished. Even some people he has never met before, he will approach after a few minutes.

And he long ago graduated from Blanket Hour. He has become secure enough that he spends a lot of time lying on the couch in the living room with the big dogs. He can still hear the troubled waters rushing below a little bit, but for all intents and purposes, he knows he's crossed over them safely and is on high ground, so to speak. On high ground is where all dogs deserve to be.

Still, it always just hurts your heart wondering how anybody could abuse an animal to the point that it quakes in people's presence and can't even allow itself to be held for comfort. Why would anyone trample over a voiceless, powerless dog's right to live in peace and know love without fear? Why would anyone abandon an animal with the capacity to love? Why would anyone cause a dog to become so traumatized it can't even follow its own instinct to be held close by someone who wants to make its life better?

It took months and months for Cotton *(left)* to warm up to the idea of Blanket Hour. But he finally did. Here he is snuggling on a blanket with Danny and Moose, a little dog we rescued from a shelter.

Chapter 8

We Will Survive

Ron was shuffling papers around while sitting on one of the stools at the kitchen island, absentmindedly stroking Milly's ear while he looked over bills that had come in, trying to figure out which ones could wait. In her old age, the charcoal-hued Katrina rescue had begun seeking out a little more attention and affection, and she liked that Ron could acknowledge her and let her know he cared about her without really paying her direct attention. That would have been more focus on her than she could have been comfortable with.

It had been almost five years since the hundred-dollar check had come in once we had officially become a nonprofit rescue organization. Encouraged by that first glimmer of success as a bona fide nonprofit, we ran out and bought fancy blank cards to write thank-you notes to contributors. And truth be told, our ability to help take care of dogs did in fact increase over that time.

Some wonderful people in the horse world with significant resources started giving substantial sums; the tax write-off they could take now that we were a 501(c)3 allowed them to donate more generously. Also, the more dogs we adopted out, the more contributions that came in from the adopters themselves—not payment for their new pets, just checks to help us out. The joy their Danny & Ron dogs had given them made them want to pay it forward.

We also raised funds through an annual Lip Sync event that we had started putting on during the Winter Equestrian Festival in Wellington. Kim Kolloff, a fellow equestrian, gave us the idea and helped get it off the ground.

We had never crossed paths with Kim before, but she was bothered by the fact that all the events, all the fundraisers, that took place during the Winter Equestrian Festival each year were for adults even though thousands of kids both ride and show horses during the festival and are a big part of the activities.

She wanted a charity event for *them,* not only so there would be something for them to participate in but also so they could learn about giving back, about raising money for a cause. "I always thought that if kids gave from their hearts," Kim says, "it would enrich their lives.

"I didn't know what the charity should be, but then somebody told me about Danny & Ron's Rescue, and once I met them, I knew hands down *that* was the charity. Walking into their house and seeing all the formerly abused dogs—so many of them taken away from their owners by the courts after having been neglected, starved, beaten—there was no way it wasn't going to be them.

"I had a very tough childhood, growing up in a household with abuse, neglect, and alcoholism. We had dogs, and when things were bad, the dogs were who I hugged, who I felt safe with. I knew they wouldn't turn around and hit me.

"Thankfully most children don't experience what I did, but most kids do go through things. They know about people being mean, and sometimes even abusive, and they could bring the empathy that comes from their experiences to dogs. Children and dogs all start out with unconditional love—innocent, trusting—and having that connection allows kids to be there for an animal who has been through something. It makes them feel, 'I can change this dog's life.' It empowers them to help. Also, doing something for others takes away from troubles they might be having by putting their minds on what others are going through.

"When a child holds an abused, sad dog," Kim says, "they let the dog just nestle in their arms and you can see the empathy in their faces. And dogs, for their part, understand that children are children and respond to *them* with kindness, with patience. One little Danny-and-Ron dog that was at a booth they had at the horse show," she says, "was cowering way at the back of her crate when a little girl came by to look at her. The dog was so afraid of anyone coming near her. The family she had been taken from used to kick her, leave her chained up outside. And then that girl—the face on that child, just hurting and wanting to hold the dog. She kept her arms open, and we were able to put the animal in them, and I am telling you, that dog melted in her embrace, and the child felt so . . . whole. In what other situation would a child be able to put to such good use that kind of empathy?"

But how to create a charity function by bringing children into it? A lip sync, Kim believed, would be the perfect kind of event for kids—singing, dancing, and costumes, all of it to imitate their favorite singers and bands. And she wanted it to be a competition— best outfits, best lip-syncing, and so on. There would be a Battle of the Barns, too. Kids from different horse barns would form teams to compete. Winners would receive trophies. We decided to hold the show on the Sunday evening before Presidents' Day because it would run late but everyone would be off from school the next day.

Money would be raised in two ways. One, attendees would have to buy seats to attend. And two, the children would come up with ways to raise money for Danny & Ron's Rescue on the side. Teams engaged in golf cart washes, dog washes, boot shining, bake sales—whatever they could think of to bring in money to support the dogs they had come to care so much about. They made the fundraising a competition, too, seeing who could bring in the most contributions.

The first couple of years, it was a bit of a rinky-dink operation. "I went and got some plywood, made a little stage, and put up some clip lights," Ron recalls. The audience consisted of maybe twenty-five people. But as the Lip Sync evolved and began gaining in popularity, he recounts, "we started renting a full stage and having people come in to do professional lighting." People would buy up whole tables to watch the kids "do" Madonna, scenes from *Annie*, the star-studded *We Are the World* extravaganza, and other acts. And their costumes, their talent, only increased from year to year.

Better still, Kim adds, many of the kids became involved in dog rescue all year long. They would hold bake sales and other fundraisers in their neighborhoods back home. And like that little girl trusted by the dog who started out at the back of the cage, they would come by the Danny & Ron dog booth at the Winter Equestrian Festival to hold rescues we were showcasing for adoption, help out, and learn about homeless animals. "Danny and Ron would teach them about puppy mills, about dog fighting. Kids really need to know the truth. It opens up their hearts," Kim says. "The dogs change the kids' lives as much as the kids change theirs."

The icing on the cake was the close friendship we developed with Kim. It is hard to have a conversation with her and not come away in a better mood. Her enthusiasm, her positive attitude with all she has been through, including tribulations with MS that have left her needing a wheelchair at times, are truly inspirational. Everyone can take a page out of Kim's book to live a better, less grumpy, more appreciative life.

Kim, for her part, says, "These two men have taught me so much about the love they give to animals. I call them the dog angels. There are no two people who have a heart like they do. They get phone calls throughout *every single day*. 'Somebody wants to put this dog down. That dog needs surgery.' They just say 'Yes yes yes' all day long.

"But it's not just that. I can't tell you about the love they give for *me*. They would drop everything in a minute to do anything for me. Seriously, they have become my family. I had a mass on my kidney, and Ron called me and said, 'If you need a kidney, I'm giving you mine.' It's not just me. They are as giving to people in general as they are to animals. I never met anybody like them. I am so lucky, and I'm just so grateful. I feel that I have a forever home with them. *I'm one of their rescues*."

All of those good feelings between us also bore fruit directly, and not just in terms of the added joy that comes with meaningful friendships. The annual Lip Sync event that we wouldn't have had without Kim added significantly to our annual coffers. Within a few years the audience totaled five hundred people, and Lip Sync became the most popular soiree at the Winter Equestrian Festival.

Still, no matter what, our financial responsibilities always outpaced our funds. They were never enough to make ends meet. It was our own doing. As more money came in, we kept growing the rescue, taking in more dogs and hiring staff to tend to them so they could receive the care they needed; we were approaching Katrina levels of dog care, and there was no way we could sustain that indefinitely without help. And that help—five or six people by that point—needed salaries; they needed workmen's comp.

Of course, with more dogs, there are also more surgeries, more illnesses, not to mention more food required. We had to build an addition onto the house, too. We were actually beyond the number of dogs we'd had at any one time even during Katrina, and there simply wasn't room for all of them within the square footage we had. We were glad to be rescuing greater numbers of dogs, but we needed to have space to put them. Our board, which was growing, would say to us, "You guys have to learn to sometimes say the word 'no.'" But that has never been an easy word for us when someone is in dire need. We can't just turn our backs.

We know we can't save every dog, but when someone contacts you and says, "A dog was hit by a car and is lying at the side of the interstate—can you guys go and pick it up?" we're not going to say no. Even though we were now a nonprofit business, we could not run on a business *model*.

We feel it is our mission to rescue dogs. It is why we're here.

Which is the reason Ron was sorting through bills in the kitchen even though more money was coming in. "I was losing sleep over it," he says. "I'm a very structured person— structured in life and structured financially because I was raised by Depression-era parents. I was continuously told, 'Don't owe money.' Mom and Dad always paid cash for their cars, nothing on credit. And we had a massive garden with tomato plants, pepper plants, cucumbers, and corn that my sister and I had to weed for two hours a day during summer vacations. If it rained, we weeded four hours the next day. And if it was hot, we were told to get up early and do it to beat the heat.

"My sister and I made tomato paste from harvesting those vegetables—also tomato juice, tomato sauce, dill pickles. We'd cut corn from the cob and put it into bags to freeze for the winter. Anything to make ends meet.

"So it killed me to owe money. I never wanted to get into debt. That's why, if we couldn't make payroll, couldn't pay the vet bills, we'd kick in money out of our own earnings training horses and riders, so the rescue wouldn't be in the red. But we didn't always have enough, which was why sometimes I'd have to go and get a home-improvement loan. I'd tell the bank I needed $50,000 to remodel something in the house, and then we'd use it for the dogs. We had to be able to come up with a way to make it work without sacrificing any of the animals. Then we'd chisel away at the loans, trying to pay down a little of them when more money would come in from horse training."

"I hated to see Ron going over the bills," Danny says. "I'm terrible with money, but I loathe the times when everything is on his back and he has to try to figure out how to do it. And so many times with dogs there are expenses that you don't expect. Things have to be done, and you can't put them off. It was a good feeling to know we were saving and placing dogs, but at the same time I knew our finances were going lower and lower, and it was scary. You expect as you're growing older that life should be getting a little simpler, a little easier. But it wasn't."

Then Ron received a phone call—from Gloria Gaynor. "I was just kind of stunned," he says. "It's the kind of call where you don't believe at first that the person is who they say they are."

It turned out a group of girls—sisters between the ages of eight and fifteen—were going to lip-sync to her iconic song "I Will Survive," and had written to let her know and to ask if she would be interested in making a donation because they were trying to raise money to save dogs.

Well, Gloria, as we soon came to call her, did the kids one better. Having read about Danny & Ron's Rescue from materials the girls sent her, she offered to come and help judge the Lip Sync acts for us—*and perform!*

"I'm an animal person—always have been," Gloria says, "so rescuing dogs is one of my causes as well. When we were kids, my mother got us a dog, and when the dog passed away my brothers and sister and I were so distraught, but I was more distraught than anyone else. Devastated." Gloria was also tickled, she notes, by the fact that one of her brothers is named Ron, and her father's name was Daniel.

Still, says Danny, "I didn't really believe it was going to happen. I was in disbelief. I thought, just to get the logistics worked out and for her to be free the night we needed her was going to be impossible."

But possible it was. Tickets sold out weeks and weeks in advance.

To kick the event into high gear, we brainstormed with Kim and decided to make the entire theme of Lip Sync that year a disco extravaganza, with shimmery mirror balls and strobe lights. And we asked all the attendees—those who were buying tickets to attend—to wear disco clothes.

Everybody complied. The guys, some in wigs of big, curly '70s hair, wore shiny shirts and white pants. The women wore sequins and lamé. We rented a huge tent for the occasion. And as soon as Gloria began singing—*"At first I was afraid, I was petrified"*—no one in the room was sitting anymore. She literally brought the house to its feet. Even the young children, seven, eight, nine years old, although they were generations away from disco, knew the song and were singing and dancing along with her. By the time Gloria was asking those famous questions, *"You think I'd crumble? You think I'd lay down and die?"* the crowd was beside itself.

The song couldn't have been more perfect for the occasion, and not just because it was such a hit. It linked directly to the dogs, so many of which survive abuse or other horrific situations, and many of which are plucked by us from Death Row because a shelter can no longer take care of them and no one will adopt them. Our aim, particularly with the scared ones who might have a tendency to act aggressively, is to make them lovable so they can be adopted out to a forever home. And there it was, right in the lyrics: *". . . as long as I know how to love, I know I'll stay alive."*

Of course, the song had meaning for us, too. The rescue would in fact survive, one way or another. Star power like Gloria's could only help. We saw that immediately. Posting some photos of us and Gloria together right after the event lit up our social media channels, with people gushing and commenting. That kind of public relations coup would only up our game and draw more attention to our efforts to save homeless dogs, rehabilitate them, and adopt them out.

But it went well beyond that. What we could not have known that night under the tent was that another true, solid friendship was taking root.

The very next day, Gloria joined us at the ongoing Winter Equestrian Festival and spent time talking with us. She was making a documentary of herself at the time and asked if her film crew could take some shots of the three of us chatting. We thought that was great in itself, but she kept in touch, and over time, we became part of one another's lives.

She even came back to the annual Lip Sync a second time. "The first event—that was so much fun to see the kids," Gloria says. "Oh my God, they were so precocious! It was just wonderful to watch them performing. There were a couple of them that I would expect to go on to become entertainers. And the pride in their parents—it was a wonderful way to raise money for the cause."

At her second Lip Sync visit, Gloria performed "Day One" from her twentieth studio album, *Testimony*. A beautiful, stirring song, on one level it's about going back to falling in love for the first time. But it's also a transcendent ode to baptism, about love for God, about spiritual awakening.

The album went on to win a Grammy for Best Roots Gospel Album, and Gloria honored us by including us in a small launch party for it in Nashville. She had also invited us when "I Will Survive" was inducted into the Library of Congress; she put her thumbprint right next to George Gershwin's, for "Summertime."

She was the only person ever invited to give a concert at the

Library of Congress. There was even a giant disco ball out front. Hours before the concert started, a line of people wrapped completely around the huge building, thirty-eight times bigger than the White House. But Gloria's manager, Stephanie Gold, with whom we have also become good friends over the years, gave us special passes so we could get in early. We sat right next to Stephanie backstage as Gloria was interviewed by Robin Roberts for an HBO special. It was such a special privilege to be treated by Gloria and Stephanie like that and to have an opportunity to meet Gloria's family and friends.

Gloria has also directly benefited the dogs over the years by donating proceeds from sales of "I Will Survive" memorabilia to Danny & Ron's Rescue—T-shirts and such. When the COVID pandemic started, she sold a line of "I Will Survive" masks and made donations to our rescue from that.

But the most wonderful part of our relationship with Gloria is not the name recognition she has lent the rescue nor the money she sends our way through merchandise sales or even inviting us to special events. It's the deep, abiding closeness that she has formed with us—the fun moments and the serious times and everything in between.

One year, she was going to be performing a Christmas concert in Delray Beach, Florida, not far from Wellington and the Winter Equestrian Festival. The night before the concert, we picked her and Stephanie up from the hotel, took them to dinner at a restaurant on the beach, and asked if they wanted to see the Delray Beach Christmas tree, because the city has one of the largest artificial holiday trees in the country.

"Absolutely," Gloria said.

We found a place to park right nearby and walked over. The

tree was more than a hundred feet tall, with thousands and thousands of lights. There's actually a door in it, and you can go inside and look up to see the entire spectacle illuminated above you.

When we were looking around inside, a man came over and told us that a neat thing people like to do is take a selfie by putting your phone on the ground so it looks like the heavens are above you (which we all did together for a group shot). Then he proceeded to tell us, "By the way, the concert hall next to us—tomorrow night we've got a Christmas show, and you won't believe it, but Gloria Gaynor's coming to sing there."

Allowing ourselves a smart-ass moment, we both said, "Really?"

"Mmmmm-hmmm."

Then Danny couldn't keep it up anymore and said, "Sir, just so you know, this is Gloria Gaynor."

The guy was shocked—we thought his jaw would drop to the ground—and we all had a good laugh, after which he asked if he could have a picture with her. Then word drifted outside the tree, and Gloria had to go take photos with others. She was so gracious about it, even though it was supposed to be her quiet night.

The next evening, Gloria accommodated *us*. Our board was in Wellington to meet a new staff member we were hiring, and we were going to have a party to welcome her. But we moved the party to earlier in the day to give the board a surprise. That evening, we hired a twenty-person stretch limo to drive everyone to Delray. Everybody was using their GPS to try to figure out where we were going.

We finally arrived at a hotel and told everybody to go up to the bar and get a drink. "That's our surprise?" they asked. "Drinks at a hotel?"

"Just be patient," we told them.

Then, all of a sudden, Gloria stepped into the bar, and everyone got to meet her and crow over her, and after that she and Stephanie rode with us to the concert hall where she would be singing. It was a heady event!

There have been quiet moments, too. When Ron's mother was dying, Gloria would pray with him on the phone. "She would ask God for different things for Mom," Ron says, "and strength and healing for me. That's a very special friend. For as long as I live I will always feel indebted for that and will treasure those moments. I remember getting off the phone and feeling at peace. Gloria is truly very spiritual and gave me comfort at a time that I was hurting so badly."

Gloria explains that she is happy to be in Ron's and Danny's lives. "One of the things I saw about them early on was the sacrifices," she says. "They have made so many. They gave up their pensions to do this. They continue giving, giving . . . and doing it out of their home! They care for these animals like their own children.

"They are such caring and loving gentlemen. The things they've gone through for this cause to help these helpless animals are just heart-wrenching, and I was drawn to them for all of that. They don't just wait for people to bring them animals, either. They go seeking and searching whenever there's a natural disaster. They know there are going to be animals that are lost and uncared for. It just fills my heart; I mean it."

Gloria is not able to take a Danny & Ron dog herself because she is always on the road—mostly internationally these days. "That's the only reason I don't have one," she says. "I'm just gone all the time. And I'd hate for the dog to be missing me. They say dogs have no concept of time. But I don't think that's true."

Fortunately, Gloria does frequently get to see Parker, a dog adopted by Stephanie, who is a good friend of Gloria's in addition to being her manager. "I lost my dog right before we did the first Lip Sync," Stephanie says. "I had had a dachshund for ten years—she had diabetes and Cushing's disease. She had a very stressful, hard go of it the last three years of her life, and I thought, 'I can't do this again.'

"But then four years later, Danny and Ron posted a batch of puppies on Facebook—poodle/Maltese/Yorkie mixes—and I fell in love. Their rescue managed to take the puppies' mother when she was pregnant with them. And not just her. Many dogs were surrendered to them at the same time. Someone had been keeping multiple dogs in cages and was breeding them over and over again in their own feces.

"After the operation was shut down, we waited for the dogs' mother to give birth. She had been kept in a cage for most of her life. Then Danny and Ron held on to the puppies—four in all—for several months, until they were fully weaned and had all their shots. They got the mother a home, and that's when they posted the puppies on social media.

"I met the transporter off the New Jersey Turnpike, right by the George Washington Bridge in Fort Lee, to take one of them. Parker was a little nervous, but he came readily into my arms—and then started kissing me.

"He's so lovable. He's my little love bug in bed at night, and we go bike riding every day. I have a little seat on my bike for him. He really enjoys that. And when we come back in, he tugs off my shoe, pulls out the insole, and runs around with it.

"And he *loves* Gloria. He likes nothing better than to sit on her lap, which she always lets him do. To think that if it hadn't been for Danny and Ron, he might have had a terrible life in a cage, or he might not have even survived."

Of course, with Gloria and Stephanie and Kim Kolloff's help, *the rescue* has survived, allowing dogs that people abused or neglected or "threw away" to have the happiness and security they deserved. It's a chain, and everyone is a link in it, and together we are all stronger. Gloria's book, which has the same title as this chapter, makes that very point. With others' help and dedication, we survive tough times and tribulations. Not only do we make it through but we also come out the other side empowered, and in the process make the world a better, more responsible, and more loving place.

Gloria Gaynor hanging out with a couple of dogs in our living room. The most wonderful part of our relationship with Gloria is not the name recognition she has lent the rescue nor the money she sends our way through merchandise sales or even inviting us to special events. It's the deep, abiding closeness that she has formed with us—the fun moments and the serious times and everything in between.

* * *

Ron could not be consoled. He had had Gadget almost since as far back as Katrina. Gadget belonged to both of us, of course, but the wire-haired Jack Russell terrier—black, tan, and white—stole Ron's heart when he was barely eight weeks old, sleeping in the bed right next to him and going everywhere with him.

"He was my sidekick," Ron says. "I could clap, and he would jump into my arms. He would do Bang Bang; he would drop to the ground for you. And he was super affectionate, super loyal. Very smart, too. I used to take him to some of the Jack Russell trials, where he would do the go-to-ground. It's a maze of underground tunnels with dead ends that make you have to turn around and try a different route. The aim is for the dog to find a rat in a cage down one of the 'corridors' and start barking; Jack Russells were bred for capturing varmints. Gadget won a lot of those contests. But mostly I just liked him. I loved him."

So it was no surprise that when we took him to Atlanta for a horse show and Gadget fell to the ground one day without warning, Ron went into panic mode.

"He was all of a sudden very limp and lethargic," Ron says. "He was well into his teens by that point."

Ron ran back inside with him to tell Danny what happened, then raced Gadget to a veterinary emergency room. They did some quick tests and said that somewhere internally the dog was losing blood.

Wanting to get him the best care possible, Ron put him in the car and drove to the hospital at the University of Georgia's College of Veterinary Medicine. It was about an hour and a half away, and Ron was sweating the whole time.

They took Gadget right away, did some blood work, found that he was losing blood quite quickly, and gave him plasma. Then they performed an ultrasound.

Gadget had a tumor on his spleen the size of a lemon. The emergency room doctor suggested surgery, thinking there might be a good prognosis—they could excise the tumor, Gadget would heal, and life would go back to normal. Unfortunately, a biopsy of the mass revealed that it was malignant.

Ron fell to pieces, and Danny wasn't surprised. "They were pretty much like a devoted father and son," Danny says. "They loved to play ball together—Ron could tell just by looking at him if he was in the mood for that—and Gadget always stayed by Ron's side even if he was involved with something that didn't allow him to pay Gadget any attention. It had to be completely Ron's decision about Gadget's medical treatment."

"I wasn't going to allow chemo or even radiation," Ron says. "He was just too old, and weighing the effects of the treatments, I just wanted him to have whatever quality of life he could. I knew the tumor would probably metastasize, or maybe even already had, but I didn't want to try to buy him more time with invasive treatments and running him back and forth to the doctor, which he wasn't going to appreciate in his weakened state.

"I put him on an all-organic diet in an effort to keep him as healthy as possible," Ron says, and two more seasons passed with things remaining status quo, sometimes even better than status quo.

That fall, we had some indoor horse shows at Washington International, and of course we took Gadget with us. The hotel didn't allow dogs, but, Ron says, "I didn't know how long he would be here, and I wasn't going to leave him home." The solution he came up with was to put Gadget in a duffel bag to get him up to the room and then just sneak him in and out as needed.

He was very quiet at the reception desk and remained that way when we got on the elevator. But it stopped at the very next floor, when the hotel manager joined us. It was at that moment that a brand-new tennis ball Ron had in his jacket pocket for Gadget to play with fell out and bounced around the elevator floor, as a new tennis ball will. The duffel bag started moving, and Ron started fumbling with the luggage to make it seem like it was he who was moving things around. The manager then got off at a floor below our own. Whew!

After that, getting him in and out to go to the bathroom a few times a day was quite a feat, but a piece of cake compared with the first day.

A couple of months after the show, sixteen-year-old Gadget went downhill quickly. "I knew one morning," Ron says. "He had that look in his eye—or maybe the lack of a look."

Our friend George was in town, and the three of us went together to put Gadget at peace. "I held him as he went," Ron says, "and we all cried."

But Ron cried the hardest, Danny comments. "Ron and Gadget, they were a thing, no doubt," he says.

Afterward, we went into downtown Camden for lunch, and Danny and George badgered Ron into going antiquing. It was the last thing he felt like doing—his heart was still with Gadget at the doctor's office—but they felt he needed a bit of a separation from what had happened and convinced him to browse around an antiques store with them.

The store was right next to the bus station, and when we stepped outside, a little shadow-colored miniature poodle mix, shaggy with curls, jumped up on our legs with his tail wagging. He ran around happily while his large dark eyes glinted with joy, and we all exclaimed that he was one of the cutest dogs we had ever seen, when an older man called out, "You want my Bobby?"

We looked at him, surprised.

It turned out he was up from Tallahassee doing logging work, but his truck had been totaled in an accident and he was taking the bus home. The thing was, he didn't learn until after he bought the ticket that dogs were not allowed.

"Why don't you give us your address?" Danny finally responded. "We'll keep him for you until you get settled back home, and then we'll make arrangements to have him sent back to you when you're ready."

"You gentlemen are mighty sweet," the man answered, "but if I have to leave my Bobby once, I have to leave him forever. I can't have him not trusting me for the rest of his life."

That touched us, but Ron was at first reticent, albeit just a little. "My heart was so torn from losing Gadget," he says. "The last thing I was thinking of was acquiring another dog right away. I was in a lot of pain from what had just happened."

"I'm tired. I'm old," the man said. "I've got to get home. I think you gentleman will take good care of him for me."

At that point we were all just about in tears again, Ron especially. Our distress over the day's events became rolled right up into the sadness of the man's voice as he spoke. Perhaps mistaking the forlorn look on our own faces with hesitation, he offered the following enticement: "He don't shit in the house!"

With such an irresistible temptation, what choice did we have but to take Bus Stop Bobby home with us?

Upon pulling into the driveway we took him straight to the

laundry room. He really needed a bath. But he immediately jumped up on the washer, looked out the window, and started crying pitifully for his owner, now headed south to Florida. He was absolutely heartbroken, and the crying and longing went on for three days, making us wonder if we had acted too hastily in the emotional confusion of missing Gadget. In the rush of it all, we never even took the man's contact information, so we couldn't reunite Bobby with him even if we tried.

At the time, Danny's sister Lynne didn't have a dog, and we thought filling in the hole of the mutual loneliness might help them both. We told her how cute he was (because he certainly was) and how the two of them might really bond.

Normally, she would have just said yes. But something—who knows what—stopped her, and she said she wanted to think about it. A couple of days went by and she called us back to say, "I think things happen for a reason. I think Gadget probably sent him."

There was no way Ron was going to give him up after that. And don't you know, Bobby started to sleep in the bed with us that very night, started to bond.

"He really was an amazing dog," Ron says, "as loyal as they come. He could never replace Gadget, because no one dog can truly replace another. And they were very different dogs, anyway. Gadget was a lot more playful—he would happily catch a ball or throw a stick. Bobby was more about mouthing soft toys. But he sure soothed my heart. A Velcro dog who always wanted to be with you, whether it was me or Danny, he was never interested in running off on his own adventure. He was all about being at our sides."

He had sweet, fetching ways about him, too. He was a real talker. He gave a cute little yodel-like howl when he wanted your attention, either to be petted or just to be close. He had some ador-able idiosyncrasies as well.

The golf cart that we always take to horse shows to cover all the acreage is a three-seater. The two of us sit in the front seat and let the dogs we bring along choose where they want to sit in the back two seats. Well, Bus Stop Bobby always chose the rear seat. And no other dog would jump up on it if he was there.

It wasn't like he showed the other dogs that he wanted it to himself. He hadn't decided he needed a throne; there was no ag-gression. It was just some kind of pact they all made that went under the human radar. Even if we had five or six dogs along who piled onto the golf cart along with Bobby, they would all smush together in the middle row so he could have his own space.

Bobby spent many happy years with us. Whether he ever thought about his previous owner at the bus stop, who could tell? But over time it felt as though he had never had any other home.

As he grew older, we went from taking him for veterinary well-ness visits once a year to twice a year, and on one of those visits sometime after his sixteenth birthday, the doctor told us he needed a dental cleaning under anesthesia in order to get below his gum line. (We have never had a dog who has been able to sit still and open wide.) We scheduled the appointment for the following week and then brought him in during the morning and went to do some teaching to a few horse riders; it was going to be a couple of hours.

We were out in the field when the phone rang. It was the vet. There was a large black growth in the back of Bobby's mouth. "If it's a melanoma, it can metastasize quickly," the doctor said. "Do you want me to biopsy it and send off the sample to pathology?"

We said yes and asked him to please rush it.

A few minutes later the doctor called back. On a hunch, he

had taken a lung X-ray even though he had taken one only the week before with no unusual findings. This time, however, he saw a small mass. The lungs are among the first places a tumor like the one Bobby might have would spread.

Sure enough, the pathology report came back positive for cancer, and the prognosis was grim. It was one of the fastest-spreading malignancies known and would soon reach Bobby's brain, his liver, his other organs. Yet another X-ray showed that the mass in his lung had grown to four times its size in just several days.

He was given seven to ten days to live yet was still acting like himself. They say the best way to die is to have all your illness compressed into a very short period at the end of your life, and that sure seemed to be the case with Bobby. Still, Ron cried without any ability to feel consoled. That life has to come with sorrow, with parting, is sometimes almost too much to bear.

We listened to the doctor about how at the very end Bobby could in fact end up in a great deal of pain. Ron felt that if the dog only had such a short amount of time left and was lucky enough to still be feeling good, he wanted to let him go out like a champ.

So right then and there at the doctor's office, with Danny's approbation, Ron made the decision to say goodbye, holding Bobby and hugging him while the doctor gave him the drugs that would let him cross the Rainbow Bridge right in Ron's arms. It was part of the cycle of life, a cycle that could never sidestep the devastating blow that falling in love with a dog will bring; chances are that we are going to outlive them. But Ron takes comfort, even today, in the thought that maybe Bus Stop Bobby and Gadget are on the other side together, cuddling close for company.

Chapter 9

Making It Official, Part 2

We have all heard stories of family members fighting over a will, going so far as to sue each other over a departed loved one's earthly assets. It has even been the stuff of sitcoms, although in reality it is not funny. Fights over wills tear people apart, and if there are children or pets involved, the emotional fallout spills over onto them even though they have no say in the matter.

We could never imagine either of our families ever trying to stand in the way of what we specify in our wills. We each have very close relationships with the other's relatives. Ron was particularly close with Danny's sister Lynne, a widow and the longest-lived of his three siblings. "I considered her a sister, not a sister-in-law," Ron says, "and I know she felt the same way about me. If she happened to be visiting from North Carolina when I was sick with a cold or the flu, she'd come into the bedroom and say, 'Look what I have for you, Ronnie.' She knew I found chocolate pudding very soothing.

"And if I had a medical procedure like knee surgery while Danny was off at a horse show, she came from three hours away to stay over and take care of me. Likewise, if her daughter had a dance recital, I'd drive the three hours to Wilmington alone if Danny had other commitments. We spoke by phone every single night. My parents at seven and then Lynne a little later."

Lynne spent every Thanksgiving with us in Florida, where we arrive each November to get ready for the Winter Equestrian Festival in Wellington. Each year on Thanksgiving night, because she loved Christmas so much, Ron would turn on all the outside Christmas lights that he had set up in advance—a spectacle that people came from miles around to see. The next day Ron and Lynne would always go together to pick out a tree.

So when she died unexpectedly from bronchitis complications the day before her sixty-seventh birthday one June, he was inconsolable. "I don't think I'm going to put up any Christmas lights," he said to Danny as we drove down to Florida later that year, calling on the phone because we always go in separate cars to make room both for dogs and luggage. Ron was getting more and more disconsolate as we headed south, thinking about spending the holiday without her.

Danny just listened, then called back in fifteen minutes. "I have one question for you," he said. "What would Lynne think?" Which goaded Ron into putting up the lights. "I was blessed to have known her and so very blessed to have her so deeply in my life," Ron says.

These days he pays tribute to Lynne by doting on her dog, Blizzard. Shaped like an English sheepdog but with a wiry coat like a wolfhound, she is the only dog permitted to inhabit the front room of the house. She and Lynne would stay in that bedroom when they visited, and after Lynne died and we brought Blizzard home to live with us, we wanted to make her as comfortable as possible.

At first Blizzie would wander all over, kind of aimlessly. She'd even sleep in our room sometimes. But she'd still want to eat in the front bedroom every morning, like she did with Lynne, and Ron made sure that happened. She still preferred to take naps there and get away from the other dogs, too, which Ron also made sure would happen. Now she stays in there pretty much all day—she's almost in her teens—and except for new litters of puppies and their moms, no other dog is allowed in her space. She even goes out the front door to relieve herself—she's the only dog in the house who doesn't have to use the doors at the back. She lets us know when she needs the door opened, and then we carry her back up the three steps when she's done. While she still has the strength to walk *down* stairs, she can no longer walk up them.

We usually leave HGTV on for Blizz. That was Lynne's favorite channel—she always had it on—and we like to think that the familiar sounds of *Love It or List It*, *Property Brothers*, *Hometown*, and *House Hunters* leave her feeling comforted. It definitely leaves Ron feeling comforted—kind of like having a part of Lynne there with us.

Danny has enjoyed a good relationship with Ron's family as well. Ron had been back in his parents' life shortly before we got together in 1990. Not long before he and Paige separated, his father suffered a massive heart attack. In critical condition and not knowing if he would survive, he asked to see his son for perhaps the last time despite Ron's mother refusing to talk to him.

Ron had to sleep on the floor of his father's hospital room—his mother wouldn't let him come home—but that visit cracked open the door a little bit, as Ron puts it, and after seven years of emotional abandonment by his parents, their relationship gradually healed. (And Ron's father went on to live another twenty-four years.)

Once Danny came on the scene, they never discussed what he was doing in Ron's life. But it was clear they knew—and were grateful for his presence. "We are so thankful that you two have each other," Danny says Ron's mother would tell him. "We're at so much more peace that you're there for him."

"When things like that are said," Danny comments, "you don't feel like you have to say more."

She would send Danny homemade carrot cake—his favorite—for his birthday—and batches of chocolate chip cookies with notes to Ron that playfully chided him in advance that the treats were for Danny and not for him.

Danny and Ron's mother had long talks, too. "She'd tell me different stories about her family having to escape from Lithuania under Russian occupation," he says, "and even though she was born here, I could see what made her a stoic, brave, and determined woman.

"When Ron was growing up and even in his early adulthood, there was not a lot of gray area for her. It was all black and white. But as she grew older she became more open-minded, even changing her party affiliation for the 2016 presidential election. She had always been a staunch Republican but said to me, 'Here I am approaching ninety years old, and I think I'll have to become a Democrat.' She wasn't mushy in her affections, but I felt very much like I was parented by both Mrs. D. and Mr. D., as I always called them. I felt they always tried to show me compassion and love.

"And Mrs. D. had a very soft side. Into her late eighties, she would shovel deep snow at the barn so she could go to feed the feral cats there long after Ron had removed the horses to South Carolina."

Danny has a strong relationship with Ron's sister, Diane, as well. And it's not just he who says so, relating, "We both love each other very much and share heartfelt experiences with each other quite a bit."

Echoes Diane, "I don't think I'd be able to *choose* a better relative than Danny. He is by far my favorite. He's like my other brother. He's so compassionate and caring and empathetic. Especially when I'm going through hard times, he will write really caring things about how he's thinking of me. I always look forward to getting cards from him.

"Just yesterday—I've been having some tough times with my daughter and her boyfriend—my doorbell rang, and the florist delivered beautiful hydrangeas that I could plant outside, and a wonderful spring bouquet with all kinds of flowers for inside, with a note from Danny that said, 'I hate for you to be going through this.'

"He's also probably the most nonjudgmental person I know. He always gives you the benefit of the doubt. And with all his health issues and all he's gone through, I don't think I once ever heard him complain. He helps me have a more beautiful view of life."

But for all of the mutually heartfelt feelings between each of us and the other one's relatives, we still felt after a series of talks over time that we needed to have a marriage certificate.

We each have a will that specifies all our earthly belongings go to the other one upon our death. And we also know that whoever goes first, the one who remains will look after the other's family and help out in whatever ways are needed. But there are a lot of ins and outs with wills. And until a will is settled, while it remains in probate, there can be significant limbo time. Things can happen. Wills can be contested, for instance, even by people not mentioned in them—sometimes *especially* by those people.

You can work to legally cement what's going to occur with your money by creating a trust. But trusts are not necessarily airtight, either, and also expensive to execute. And our situation is complicated, with deeds both to Ron's house and Danny's farm that would have to be taken into account along with provisions for keeping the dog rescue going in the event of our demise.

If you're married, however, your spouse becomes your closest relative, and all worldly goods automatically go to that person once you die unless your will specifically states otherwise—no matter whose name might be on a property deed or a bank account. You own together what each of you have owned individually; it all legally becomes "ours" instead of "his." That was critically important to us most of all because of the animals—not just the dogs but also the horses we keep at Danny's farm and the donkeys, cows, and other rescue animals that we take in. We keep retired horses in pastures at the house, too. And knowing what can happen to people's pets, we did not want any animal wrenched from the home where it finally knew security in order to suit anyone's desire for some kind of expediency in dissolving our estates.

There was also another legal reason we wanted to be married. We had too often experienced the frustration and emotional pain of not being able to take the lead on medical decisions for each other without permission from our sisters. Ron has had his share of hospital stays over the years just as Danny has, and getting medical teams to understand that Danny was the go-to proved as exasperating and paperwork-heavy as it did when Ron needed to see to Danny's needs during *his* hospital stays. "Every time you go to a doctor and have to fill out paperwork," Danny says, "it asks who is your first contact if anything should happen to you. It next asks 'Relationship to You,' and if you say 'friend' or 'partner,' their eyes kind of automatically go to contact number two. If you have the legal right to say 'husband' or 'spouse,' it puts a whole other light on it."

So we decided to make our union legal. That one piece of paper would close all the loops. And truth be told, it wasn't only for the purposes of documentation that would allow us to live—and die—knowing that our wishes for each other would be honored.

"As recently as thirty or forty years ago," Ron says, "people like Rock Hudson were gay but could not come out. How depressing that had to be to express your full self only in the shadows. So it would be a great step for us being gay to be able to say, 'Yes, we are married.'

"It actually made me a little sad, and to be honest, a little angry that so much of the reason we were getting married was solely for logistics. Other people are able to think of their weddings strictly in terms of declaring that they love the other person and want to spend their life with them."

Danny comments, "We felt like we wanted to solidify what we had and who we are so that it would be beyond question. 'Are they a couple? Are they not a couple?' We are, and we are proud of that and happy about it.

"There's not a better person than Ron," he adds. "He means everything to me.

"Ron likes to direct, he likes to be the authority, and he often is. It's a good thing because I'm the opposite. If things are going a little rough and we're feeling a little broke, I'll just be quiet and wait it out, but Ron will get on it. I've never known him not to have too much on his plate.

"It's not just the practical stuff. Nobody will give more of themselves than Ron when it comes to somebody in trouble or in pain or in the hospital. And he's true not only to the person in pain. He'll be like a support group for entire families. He's so good at it. Even with families where people don't get along with each other and all hell is breaking loose, he's the one who'll sit there and talk to each one. He has solved so many family crises. I try to help, too, but less directly, less hands-on.

"I think part of the dynamic is that because I've lost so many family members early, including my middle sister, Cheryl, ten years before Lynne, I realize how little control I have no matter what I do. Ron attacks life with the purpose of just getting everything done, with no obstacle too big. In fact, it was hard for me to watch him seeing his parents grow older and knowing that eventually he'd lose them. He adored his mother and father, and they adored him. You hate getting ready for someone else's pain.

"I'm not saying it's always like a sugar candy train ride. We can get pretty intense with each other at times. When you work together as well as live together, you're bound to have words here and there. But it has nothing to do with the amount of love or appreciation I have for him. I would truly be lost without him, and I'd give the world for him, *do* anything in the world for him. It hurts me when I see him hurting or stressing because of everything he does.

"A piece of paper was not going to make our relationship any stronger than it already was," Danny adds. "In our own heads we had already been married for years, decades. But it would gild the lily a little bit and help make it clear to *others* who we were."

Ron agrees. "Getting married was never going to change our relationship," he says. "Danny is my soul mate, as I've said before. He is the person I love, and a ceremony and certificate could not make my feelings any stronger. But with our getting older and doors opening more for the gay community, it would solidify not only our legal privileges together but also who we are in the eyes of the world, make it beyond question. It would make it 'for real' to people that the commitment is there."

When we made the decision, gay marriage wasn't yet legal in South Carolina. But we knew it was just a matter of time. The legalization of same-sex unions was spreading across the country. So we flew up to New York, where our marriage would already be considered legitimate, for a five-day wedding/honeymoon combination. We love Broadway musicals—we are Broadway-holics—and decided to stay in the Marriott Renaissance, right in Times Square. It would be easy to walk to all the theaters from there.

It felt odd not to have any of the dogs with us; we were so used to traveling with at least a few of them at a time. But we knew it was better to leave them at home in their comfort zone rather than take them to a hotel and then in and out to go to the bathroom. It was better to keep their lives normal rather than make them adjust to an event for us that they wouldn't understand and that wouldn't do them any good.

"I always miss feeling that warmth next to your back when we have to travel without any dogs," Ron says, "just being able to put your arm around them and talk to them when they wake up. Even now in this very minute, working on this chapter, there are twelve dogs sitting on the bed with us, watching us, looking alert when we emphasize something, and getting scratched behind the ears by us and having their bellies rubbed. They're always there."

We also worry about leaving the ones who are up in age. What if something happens when we're not there? Daisy in particular, our Katrina dog who howled like the dickens at mealtimes, was quite old by that point and in failing health. It was hard for her to get up and down.

We know all of them so well, too, inside and out. We know their every little idiosyncrasy, and we know if something's not right with them. It's not that we don't have the highest regard for the people working at the rescue, and we always leave specific instructions that they follow through on to the letter. But we ourselves know when one of them is even the slightest bit off color.

Still, for all that, leaving all the dogs at home was in their own best interest. This was going to be an elopement of sorts—just the two of us.

Truth be told, we also didn't want to make a big fuss about it with other people because of Ron's mother, who was widowed by that point. We weren't looking for people to contact her to congratulate her. While she knew we were a couple, we never discussed it openly, even sleeping in separate bedrooms when we went to visit her in Illinois. You might say it was hypocritical. But having been born in 1928 and not being an open-minded person by nature, she would have felt very uncomfortable—the world had changed a lot since she was young—and we wanted to spare her that. We knew that soon enough with all the changes afoot, parents and grandparents would be openly rejoicing in the fact that their children had found love, no matter who they found it with.

Once we arrived in Manhattan, we stood in line for two hours in a nondescript, echoey hallway in New York City's Municipal Building to fill out the application for our marriage license. We were told we could come back the next day to pick up the certificate and exchange vows, but that just didn't feel right, even for two people who were doing this largely for pragmatic reasons.

Ron did some research and found a minister who would marry us at the hotel. We chose a spot on the same floor as the hotel restaurant because it had large glass windows that directly overlooked Times Square. You could see all the billboards, the people walking. It made for an exciting backdrop in a place we loved to be.

We chose late afternoon so there wouldn't be a lot of coming and going. A bar anchored the restaurant at the far end, and whoever did come in tended to head in that direction, opposite the secluded corner we had chosen, so it felt pretty private, intimate. The minister was lovely, serving as our witness as well as our officiant and photographer. Right in front of a window, with all of humanity on the streets and the billboards lighting up as the sun began to set, she had us exchange vows and rings in a simple ceremony that took just a few minutes. She then instructed us to kiss and congratulated us on becoming spouses.

We didn't expect to have any reaction, but it really did feel special. There's something about an almost tangible affirmation of love, especially one that we never thought would be possible when we were younger, that does in fact gild the lily.

The next few days were a whirlwind of enjoying the pulse and verve of New York and taking in as many shows as we could, both matinees and evening performances. We saw everything from *Wicked* to *Jersey Boys*, *The Book of Mormon*, *Pippin* . . .

And despite missing the dogs, the first couple of nights of sleeping without them felt absolutely luxurious. So many of them love to sleep under the covers with us (we asked the rescue staff at home to please turn down the covers at nighttime instead of leaving them tightly tucked in so that the dogs' routine would not be as disrupted in our absence). Some sleep on the pillows, on our heads. Without them there, we could move, we could stretch, we could roll over without having to figure out who was underneath.

"I use a lot of pillows to prop myself up because of sleep apnea," Danny says. "With Cotton," he reports, referring to the white fluffy poodle mix, "I always feel like I'm sliding down and have my head only partly on my bottom pillow. He keeps a leg on either side of my head. The minute I roll or move in some other way, he repositions himself so that he's on top of my head again. And I hate moving him. It was a new experience not having to worry about that."

"It's amazing not to wake up with dog hair across your T-shirt and across your face," Ron says, "to start out in absolutely clean sheets that *stay* clean through the night and even be able to stretch diagonally across the bed a little bit. It's amazing to wake up in the middle of the night to go to the bathroom and not have to wedge yourself back into the bed between dogs when you're done. It's not easy to find space when you're six foot eight. You do a lot of adjusting as the dogs curl themselves back around you."

It was good to be able to get a break from the routine in general. Our day normally starts with the alarm going off at 5:30 a.m., although the barking generally begins around 5, and once it's time to get up we have to remove dogs from our heads, from our sides, from under the covers, even to reach over to the cell phone to shut the alarm and turn on the light. Then we let out the dogs who have been crated through the night because they haven't yet learned not to "go" in the house. Some have to be let out as quickly as you can open the crates because "otherwise, they'll go in their pants," as Danny puts it. They run out the doggie door to do their business and then back in for breakfast and, if necessary, medication. Many of the dogs require special meals—low-sodium, low-fat, high-fiber—and the medicines also have to be matched to the animals so that the wrong dogs don't get the wrong pills.

While Ron feeds (it amounts to 350 pounds of dog food each week), Danny often has to do some mopping up (a dog has thrown up in the night or wasn't able to wait till morning to relieve himself), transfer items from the washer to the dryer, maybe give some of the dogs their medicine with a syringe rather than via pills, and grab a cup of coffee as he moves about. Certain dogs have to be recrated through all this so they don't take another dog's food or medicine.

By 6:45, the house is no longer ours. Staff comes in and starts picking up bowls and finishes the feeding routine while we each take quick showers so we can drive over to the farm and start our day job training horses and riders. Before the equestrian training actually begins, we feed the chickens, cows, non-show horses, and mules with things we've prepared at home. It's not their meals. Staff at the farm gives them their rations, as well as feeding the larger dogs there. It's treats—fruits like melon that we cut up for the chickens, sometimes squash, even leftover bits of casserole; apples and other things for the cows and horses; carrots for the rescued mules.

It's not that the animals require treats. But we enjoy it when they come up to the fence to greet us, and we want them to feel comfortable and to like us. We want them to feel like they have a home rather than are just a "product." The horses who have been rescued may never have had a good life before, and this is their opportunity to enjoy one. Retired show horses who used to get treats all the time still need to feel valued even though they don't perform anymore, and along with giving them treats we put fans in their turnout sheds to blow on them during the hot southern summers. The cows, too, need some interaction.

Once we feed the animals and spend several hours training show horses to earn our living, it's back to the house, perhaps picking up some items first on the way home, maybe some fencing from Lowe's or a few groceries. We also try to get a quick bite to eat as we don't really have time for a decent breakfast.

In the afternoons, after Ron makes notes of progress with the show horses for our clients, we run dogs to the vet and take calls from shelters with emergency situations, then drive over and pick up dogs with medical problems requiring immediate attention that the shelters cannot afford to cover.

Around 6 o'clock, Ron cooks dinner while making his way around staff in the kitchen who are pulling things together for the dogs' evening provisions.

It's a lot. Each day is crammed. Still, for all that, after a couple of nights in New York we started to miss the comfort the dogs and the other animals provide us, perhaps something like what couples feel when they leave the kids at home. We got a little of what we needed when we saw a panhandler sitting at the corner of Broadway and Thirty-Sixth Street with a black mutt. Probably weighing about forty pounds, the dog was so docile and submissive, avoiding all eye contact and not even really acknowledging people walking by.

Seeing a homeless person is difficult enough, but seeing him with a dog. . . . We stopped and chatted a little bit while stroking the pet on his muzzle.

The man told us, "This dog is my family." We gave him $100 and said that he should use some of it on himself but that we wanted to make sure his dog got fed.

Suckers, maybe, but it comforted us to think that perhaps we were helping that poor gentleman and his companion.

Finally, it was time to fly home and stroke the dogs in our own care. A great scampering of paws greeted us upon our arrival, with a number of the dogs jumping up on us and lots of barking. Through the cacophony came Daisy's yodel: "Where is my food?!" It was as if she hadn't been fed the entire time we were away.

The night we arrived back, our bed was once again abuzz with canine closeness and emotion—and relief—and by the next morning we were back to 5:30 a.m. feedings, training horses till noon, and tending to the veterinary, behavioral, and other needs of the dogs in the afternoon and evening.

In other words, on one level nothing had changed. But on another gigantic, almost cosmic, level, everything had.

No union is more profound than marriage, for it embodies the highest ideals of love, fidelity, devotion, sacrifice, and family. In forming a marital union, two people become something greater than once they were. As some of the petitioners . . . demonstrate, marriage embodies a love that may endure even past death. It would misunderstand these men and women to say they disrespect the idea of marriage. Their plea is that they do respect it, respect it so deeply that they seek to find its fulfillment for themselves. Their hope is not to be condemned to live in loneliness, excluded from one of civilization's oldest institutions. They ask for equal dignity in the eyes of the law. The Constitution grants them that right.

Justice Anthony Kennedy, writing for the majority of the Supreme Court, which voted to strike down once and for all a law that was said to create "a stigma" and "humiliate" by allowing individual states the ability to ban same-sex marriage.

Chapter 10

Smoke

Milton's hair was so tangled that his front legs were matted together. So were his hind limbs. Not that it mattered much; he didn't have the strength to walk, anyway. Through the matting we could see a lot of red, bloody serum oozing out of him. And there was an awful odor. We suspected he had some kind of deep infection, an abscess somewhere. He was lethargic, too, as limp as a dishrag.

The local shelter had picked up the tan-colored shih tzu mix on the side of the road and called us as a last-ditch effort before putting him down. It wasn't clear if he was a stray or if someone had thrown him out of their car. How long he had languished there was anybody's guess. It was early April, and chances were he had suffered some uncomfortable days since the tail end of winter.

From the shelter we raced Milton over to the veterinary clinic. "He is dying," the doctor told us. His temperature was 76, when a dog's normal temperature hovers between 100 and 102.5 degrees. "His organs are shutting down," the vet said. "What do you want me to do?"

"Try to save him," we answered.

"If a sick dog has gone 'inward' and is denying any part of living, then they probably should be let go," Ron says, "but a lot of them don't want to go yet." That was the case with Milton, sick as he was.

When we went to pet him after arriving at the shelter, his tail went thump thump, and he rolled over a little so we could stroke his belly. "He didn't realize that whatever he had been put through was supposed to make him fearful or despondent or hopeless or too drained to want to live," Danny says. "He was ready to interact, and nobody was a stranger to him."

"If there's still a little glint in their eye," Ron adds, "we won't give up. That's our promise to the animals. Once we take them on, we treat them like our personal dogs, so unless it's unfair to the dog we'll do everything in our power to save him."

When the vet clipped Milton's front legs apart, we could see straight through to his tendons, bones, and flesh, all crawling with maggots. There was no skin left—the mats of hair were actually strangulating it, cutting off the blood supply and causing his skin to rot, which contributed to the awful odor. In addition, he was so flea- and tick-infested that he had frank anemia; he needed a couple of pints of blood. And his white blood cell count was extremely elevated, indicating that an infection was raging.

Every single day we receive phone calls and texts about homeless and other at-risk dogs like Milton, always asking if we want to take them. We also receive throughout each week about 150 e-mails with "Code Red" lists from various shelters. The dogs on those lists are going to be put down very shortly if someone doesn't adopt them. Since we receive 300 to 500 e-mails daily and barely have time to go through them, we tend to reserve Sunday nights for making our way through the Code Reds.

The particular lists we receive add up to some 800 dogs on Death Row, and we have the unenviable task of figuring out which ones we should look into saving. Of course, a dog like Milton ends up high on our list of dogs to check out. He was going to be put down the very next day.

We virtually never pull the dogs who are impossibly cute—the adorably fluffy ones who have great personalities and no health issues. They have the best chance of any animal in a shelter of someone falling in love with them at the eleventh hour and taking them home.

Instead, we take the mopey or scared ones who don't come to the front of the cage wagging their tails, with the hope of rehabilitating them so that they will learn to bask in the embrace of a loving household that eventually adopts them. We take the ill. So many people wouldn't even think of adopting a dog who has tested positive for heartworm, for instance, and shelters don't want to hold on to them. They're often at the top of euthanasia lists. But heartworm is so easy to resolve with medication, and the dogs it tends to affect are innocent one- and two-year-olds, full of life and ready to have fun and bring joy to a family. Yet it's going to be over for them for something that wasn't their fault, which is why we step in when we can.

Misty, another dog we were contacted about, was one of the mopey, fearful ones. She was surrendered by her owners because they were moving and didn't want to take her with them. That happens a lot. People change residences and want to "start fresh," so they dump their dog at a shelter. Or they have children and no longer feel they can devote time to their dog so they unload it. For too many people, a dog is not a family member but a disposable trinket.

"Misty is completely petrified," the shelter director told us. "She is adorable, but she will not come out of the corner of her pen. Also, she looks exactly like Ebenezer." The woman remembered the miniature dachshund from years earlier and hoped Danny's feelings for Nezer would drive the decision. The shelter happened to be particularly crowded when Misty arrived because there had been a bust on a dog-fighting ring, and all the dogs who ended up there had to be housed separately in individual runs because they had been taught to be violent toward other dogs. They were also going to be there for a while on a judicial hold—a court case was going to decide whether they were the property of the shelter or should be given back to their owners. Issues of ownership can become very complicated in situations like that, even while to us it is cut and dry that dogs used for gambling in fighting rings should never be given back to their owners.

Danny went down to the shelter to have a look at Misty. He wasn't at all sure—and not because she turned out not to look anything like Nezer. "I felt reluctant because while she was so withdrawn, she was awfully sweet-looking—a little cocker spaniel mix—and she wasn't on the immediate euthanasia list so I figured somebody would take her, and she'd come out of her shell in the comfort of a new home."

While he was deliberating, a second dog in the pen, a smallish husky mix, kept coming up to him and putting her paw on him, giving him a lick or two with each approach. Then someone who worked at the shelter came and grabbed her.

"Where are you going with her?" Danny asked.

"We're going to euthanize her," the shelter worker replied. "She's bitten a couple of people, and we can't rightfully adopt her out."

It turned out it was the dog's third time back at the shelter. She lived with a couple, and every time the husband would get angry at the wife, he would abuse the animal. He hit her with things, beat her, and then would drop her at the shelter, after which the wife would come and take her back home. For all we know, given the odds, he abused his wife, too. By one estimate compiled by the National Coalition Against Domestic Violence and the American Humane Association, more than 70 percent of pet-owning female partners who eventually find safety at a woman's shelter report that their abuser also injured, maimed, killed, or threatened family pets for revenge or to psychologically control.

In any event, the last time the husband laid a hand on the animal he must have beaten her mercilessly. We assume the violence is what had turned the little dog into a biter. Almost always, dogs bite out of fear, and that was the case with this one.

Danny immediately ran up to the front desk and told the administrator on duty that he would take the animal. "She had such beautiful eyes, and she was responding to me just fine," he says.

The administrator told him they couldn't let him have her

because they didn't want to be liable if she bit him, to which he responded, "Fill out the paperwork. She's coming with me."

"Danny is go-with-the-flow," Ron says, "but not when it comes to an animal's safety or well-being."

Danny ended up taking Misty, too. While she wasn't slated to be put down right away, the shelter at that time had a 90 percent euthanasia rate; he just wasn't going to risk it. "They get so overburdened," he says, "bursting at the seams, not just with dogs but also cats, birds, rabbits. At some point they have to cull the herd."

While he was driving home, Ron called to see how it was going. "Does the dog really look like Nezer?" he asked.

"No," Danny replied, "but I have her." Long pause.

"What aren't you telling me?" Ron asked.

This is a frequent refrain for us. One of us goes to a shelter to pick up a dog and comes home with more. Or one of us can't reach the other one on the phone because he is at a shelter picking up dogs without having discussed it first.

It turned out the husky crossbreed was named Olivia—the same name as the detective played by Mariska Hargitay in her breakout role on *Law and Order: Special Victims Unit*. Living with us was going to be little Olivia's breakout role.

We no sooner got Olivia and Misty situated at the house than Misty was adopted by a family nearby. We weren't surprised. She really was a beautiful, soulful dog, and within just a few days her new family was letting us know how lovable she was and how readily she was adapting to the good life in her new home.

Olivia was a bit of a different story. She took to Ron very quickly, just as she had with Danny. But she became ferocious and defensive if anyone else so much as walked near her—to the point that when we left town for horse shows, we took her with us because we didn't trust her alone with the staff. They were fine with that arrangement. She scared them—and had bitten a couple of times, too. A little dog might not have the same clenching power of a larger one, but while a person's bite has the force of about 120 pounds per square inch, even a smallish dog can have a bite force of twice that intensity. It can do serious damage, in addition to really hurting.

At the horse shows themselves, we had to tell people not to approach our golf cart to mingle with the dogs. Olivia was very scared, particularly of men with hats. The man who had abused her wore a cowboy hat, and if anybody wearing a cowboy hat came over, the fur on her neck and back would go up (she literally raised her hackles, an automatic response to a surge of adrenaline), and then she'd stiffen and bare her teeth. It took a long, long time for her to start to be able to trust people, and even then, it was a hit-and-miss kind of thing.

Olivia did, however, get on well with other dogs, especially Bus Stop Bobby. She never sat on the back seat of the golf cart with Bobby. As you'll recall, all the dogs had made some kind of a pact with one another that the back seat was for Bobby and Bobby alone, and Olivia stuck to that. But Olivia was definitely Bobby's best friend. Inseparable, the two would sleep together, cuddle together, run and play together, and even clean each other's face and ears. We decided to keep Olivia, one, because we couldn't be sure we were going to be able to vouch that she wouldn't bite again, and two, because it would have been cruel to separate the two dogs.

Things went a little differently for Milton. After the veterinarian cut the hairs that were binding his legs together and saw what was going on, he was immediately placed on an IV drip so he could receive large doses of antibiotics intravenously that he wouldn't have been able to get by mouth. It was touch-and-go the first few days—he had a very rough time of it, especially being so hypothermic, and it wasn't at all clear whether he was going to come around. He was so emaciated that his body was feeding off his organs, the doctor said.

By around the third day, we started seeing some improvement—there was a little more brightness in his eyes, a little more activity. At the shelter, he had barely been able to stand.

Three and a half weeks he remained in the hospital, and we did not miss a single day of going to see him. Just as he had thump-thumped his tail at the shelter, he eagerly came to the front of his cage to see us and was happy to be held by us once the doctor said it was okay. His infection was healing, and new, healthy tissue was beginning to form and close over his exposed tendons and bones. His vitals started improving, too, as did his appetite, although he had to be given very small amounts of food at first because his gastrointestinal tract had remained in neutral for so long that it took time for his stomach and other GI organs to get back into gear. He started with a tablespoon of food every three or four hours, and the portion sizes increased from there.

After almost a month at the clinic, he was able to continue his recovery at the doghouse. We had to keep cleaning his wounds and continue with new doses of antibiotics, and we kept him isolated in the Q-room, or quarantine room, because he didn't have the strength to cavort with the other dogs. But as the months wore on—it was summer by that point—his flesh grew back to the point that there were only some scars, and they were hidden by his somewhat wavy hair.

By the time we let him meet his housemates, he was more

than ready. Starting out in the kitchen with the little ones, he did quite well. He loved meeting all his new canine friends, and they loved him. The staff fell in love with him, too.

By September he was ready to travel with us to the Middleburg Classic Horse Show in Leesburg, Virginia, about forty miles outside Washington, DC. We had become completely besotted with him but knew we had to let him go. He was now in great shape physically and loved being with people. It wouldn't have been fair to keep him in a home with so many other dogs, where he wouldn't get the individualized attention he deserved. People always ask us, "How can you let them go?" But how could we not, if they have a chance at a better life than the one we would be able to give them?

The agent of change at Middleburg was a ten-year-old girl named Fielding Stichman, a budding equestrian. "I saw this tent filled with all these different dogs," she says, "and I knew right away that I wanted to bring him home. I don't really know what drew me to him."

Her mother, Shannon, posits that maybe it was because "Milton was just so cute and fluffy and had a little crank in his tail," making it kind of crooked, like an old-fashioned crank handle. "He was just such a sweet dog," she adds.

Fielding asked Danny, who was manning the dog-filled tent at that moment, if she could take Milton on a walk. He of course said yes, and she took him around the show grounds on a leash, followed by "Mom, Mom, we have to get this dog!"

Although Shannon thought Milton was adorable, she was not on board. "We're not bringing home another dog," she said. The family already had a rescue, an English pointer named Rocket—and horses and chickens, not to mention Fielding's twin brother and her older brother, too.

Then she heard Milton's back story, the state he was in when he came into our hands. Fielding already had learned it and, Shannon says, "I think that's another thing that took hold of her—this awful situation that this beautiful animal had been in. She wanted to take care of him and give him a good home after everything he had been through."

Still, she hemmed and hawed, with even her horse trainer, Snowden Clarke, egging her on. "Oh, Shannon, look at him," Snowden said. "He's so cute. He's so wonderful. Of course you're not going to not take him."

"I just need to think about it," Shannon responded, but then, like the other half of Snowden's tag team, Fielding kept at it. "She was very persistent," Shannon says. "And I could see how the two of them took to each other.

"Also, I'm the kind of person who thinks, 'You need a meal? Come over.' So I realized, why *wouldn't* I take this dog? Why *wouldn't* I want to give him a wonderful home? Another benefit in my mind was that Milton wasn't a puppy. We weren't going to have to put in months of work training him."

"What are we going to tell everyone at home?" Fielding asked, once her mother had made the decision to adopt Milton.

"We're not going to say anything," Shannon answered. "We're going to walk into the house with Milton and just pretend like he was always in the family."

"When we came home," Shannon says, "my husband, Bennett, asked, 'Who's this?' I responded, 'That's Milton. You know Milton,' like, what do you mean? Stop being silly. Then I asked him to get the bags out of the car."

And that's how Milton became a member of the Stichman family. In truth, Shannon says, "Bennett is kind of used to the stuff I—I don't want to say 'pull,' but that I just kind of *do*." Which became totally clear when Shannon told us the story of how he came home one day to find what Shannon calls "beautiful orange ducks" swimming in the family pool.

Once Milton settled in, the family learned his quirks. When out for a walk, he'd just sit down after a while and refuse to move. That's enough, his obstinacy said. "We'd have to carry him back," Shannon comments. Also, heaven help you if you tried to take a bone from him. One time he got hold of a chicken bone, and Shannon went to pull it out of his mouth so he wouldn't end up swallowing a piece of it and potentially cause an obstruction farther down his gastrointestinal tract. She ended up needing to use tongs to wrest it from him without getting hurt in the process.

But these were just his ways, Shannon explains, not things the family found truly frustrating or exasperating. And Milton and Fielding, for their part, went on to continue to develop the amazing connection that had started back at the tent on the horse show grounds. Even when she first brought him back to Danny, he wouldn't leave her side to play with the other dogs. And when she sat cross-legged on the ground to make it easier to pet him, he hopped in her lap. "I think sometimes dogs choose *you*," Shannon says. "They feel safe with you. They know you're the person who's going to take care of them, love them, protect them. It did seem like Milton chose Fielding just as much as she chose him."

The two became very much an item at home. Milton got on with everyone, for sure. Even Rocket didn't mind him, although they didn't snuggle up together, and Milton would have liked Rocket to be more of a playmate rather than the aloof dog he was. But for as much as the entire family enjoyed Milton's company— "He had the sweetest face, and was such a *happy* dog," Shannon says—it was Fielding he was most excited about. "He slept with her," Shannon comments. "He was her dog, without a doubt."

We are thrilled that Milton was able to go on to have a wonderful life in such a loving home. And Olivia, the dog found with Misty that Danny took back to the doghouse with him—she, too, has had such a happy, secure life with us. But, of course, we are able to rescue only a small number of those dogs slated for euthanasia. Many go from shelters straight to their deaths.

In our area, there was a time when euthanized dogs were put in large plastic garbage bags and thrown into an open landfill. It was destroying local wildlife. Hawks would come and rip open the bags, feed on the dead dogs, and get sick and die from ingesting the euthanasia drugs still in their bodies. Other animals would feed off the birds, and the cycle would continue.

We were glad to finally see the construction of a crematorium. It protects area animals while hundreds of dogs who didn't do anything to anyone—didn't ask to be born and just needed a break—continue to be put down every week. You can see the smoke rising from the crematorium chimney on Monday evenings.

Above left: When we first saw Milton, his hair was so matted that his limbs were tangled together. He could barely walk. *Above right:* After several months of healing from a serious infection, hypothermia, flea and tick infestation, severe blood loss, and treatment for literally rotted skin, Milton was finally ready to be adopted into a loving home.

"We're not bringing home another dog," said Fielding Stichman's mother, Shannon. Guess how that worked out.

Chapter 11

On the Road

Cookie was on the move—but not because Ron wanted her to be. He had become more than a little attached to the cocker spaniel with the silky auburn hair who wasn't even quite out of puppyhood, and he wanted to hold on to her as one of our forever dogs. The demure, quiet soul would sit on his lap and melt into him as he stroked her ears, the side of her face. Making the pull even stronger was that she had come from such an awful situation, having been abandoned in a foreclosed home—no food, no furniture, no nothing. The people just up and left.

But Danny stood firm. "Ron," he said, "you know that Ylva and Jeff will give her the kind of home she deserves, without having to make her compete with a hundred other dogs for attention."

Ron knew he was right. So after he stroked Cookie's long ears one last time with his eyes brimming, off Cookie finally went with Danny on a flight out west to take her to Ylva Aberg, a massage therapist for horse riders, and her partner Jeff Gilbert, a horse show announcer with such a deep, dulcet voice that you'd be happy for him to read you a bedtime story or convince you to buy a life insurance policy you don't need.

Ylva had laid claim to Cookie the moment she saw her picture. "Jeff and I were at a horse show in Tucson," she explains, "when one of the people running the event came up to Jeff and asked if we had seen Danny and Ron's announcement that day. They had a cocker spaniel available.

"The person knew I already had a cocker spaniel—red-haired Fergie, named after the Duchess of York, and also knew I was crazy about the breed and thought I might be interested.

"The brown-eyed girl look so sweet and charming in the photo, and when I learned her name was Cookie I took it as an omen."

"Ylva had a cocker named Cookie in Sweden, before she came to the US," Jeff chimes in. "There was no way she wasn't going to take this dog."

But it took several months to get Cookie to San Diego, where Ylva and Jeff live. "We'd get on Facebook and ask if anybody was going across country and could bring Cookie with them," Ylva says. It had to be someone Danny and Ron could trust.

"She'd also call Ron every single day," Jeff reports. "'How's Cookie doing?' She wanted to make sure not only that Cookie was safe and secure but also that she would really be coming and that Ron wouldn't change his mind because he loved her so much. I said to her, 'Ylva, you don't even know this dog.' And she'd answer, 'Yes, I know this dog in my heart.'"

"The first day after I talked to Danny and Ron about taking her," Ylva says, "I went and bought her a collar and leash, even though Ron still waffled while Danny was saying yes."

Finally, after March turned to April and April to May, it turned out that Danny himself was the one who was going to put Cookie into Ylva's arms. He was flying out to San Diego for a clinic where he would teach people how to judge horse shows professionally and would bring the sweet, agreeable dog with him. She and Jeff were more than fine with that; they and Danny go back many years. "Danny doesn't let on, but he is one of the foremost authorities on hunter/jumpers," Ylva says, "one of the most respected judges and clinicians. That's aside from him being an angel."

Danny had to be careful during the trip. He was healing from a rib injury (not horse-related) and wasn't supposed to carry anything heavy. But he worked it out that he would not have to carry thirty-pound Cookie far at either end of the journey. The plan was to fly from South Carolina to Charlotte, North Carolina, and switch there for a flight that would take him straight to San Diego. The connecting plane would be at the very next gate, just steps away, so the lifting wouldn't be burdensome. But when Danny arrived in Charlotte, the gate for the next leg of the trip had been changed, and he had to maneuver with Cookie all the way to the other side of the airport.

Starting and stopping several times to give his body a rest, he finally made it to his connecting flight. But his first flight had been late—not late enough for him to miss his next plane but late enough that they had already given his seat away. It was getting on toward late afternoon by then, with options for making it out to San Diego that evening dwindling. Danny tried to wrap his head around the possibility of having to get Cookie and his luggage out to the curb for a cab to a hotel. Of course, he did not have a reservation because there had been no plan to stay over in Charlotte.

It often goes this way. Someone adopts one of our dogs but does not live anywhere near the doghouse, so the animal has to be taken by a chaperone to another part of the country to be delivered to its new family. If the dog's home is going to be on the east coast or not too far inland, it's no big deal. In fact, on the eastern side of the country, taking dogs someplace for adoption is a way of life. We are often on the road from March to November, anyway, doing horse shows from the Carolinas up into Virginia and Pennsylvania and also out to Tennessee and Kentucky, so it's easy enough to get a dog within a reasonable drive from an adopter's home. The dog generally travels with about fifteen other dogs that we take in a small bus to each show in order to try to adopt them out to equestrians or members of their families. Show attendees are used to us setting up a booth or a tent by now, and in fact, while it was once fashionable for horse show people to have purebred dogs, we are proud to say that it has become a badge of honor for those on the show circuit to have adopted a Danny & Ron dog.

Come late November, when we're down in Wellington for the Winter Equestrian Festival, dogs are there with us, too, either to be handed over to people who have already spoken for them or to be showcased for adoption. Dogs travel in the opposite direction, as well. When we're in Florida, we make it a point to take dogs from the Palm Beach County Shelter that would otherwise be put down for lack of space. And if they need rehabilitation—a dog who tests heartworm positive, for instance, and has to be on medication and carefully watched for several months until he becomes heartworm negative and finally adoptable—they are sent up to South Carolina for treatment and care.

But when it's a matter of flying rather than driving, things can become a little more complicated. One reason is that we do not let animals fly in the belly of a plane. It's just too traumatizing for them to be stowed with the luggage in a dark space and not have a clue what's going on or a person to reach down and comfort them or say some soothing words during flight. If a dog is too big to fit in the passenger cabin, someone drives to deliver the pet or to pick it up, or the two parties meet in the middle.

Another reason we don't separate dogs from chaperones is that travel snafus happen with flights, like the kind Danny was experiencing with Cookie. The last thing we'd want is for a dog to make it to a connecting flight without her person, or to accidentally be left on the tarmac for an extended period of time, especially in very hot or very cold weather. Once a dog is checked as luggage, opportunities for problems arise.

When a dog and a person are together, on the other hand, it builds in a measure of safety. And despite Danny's mishap, things usually go pretty smoothly. Like the time Ron flew west to Chicago and Nora Thomas flew east from Seattle so a Boston terrier named Maisy Daisy could be delivered safely into Nora's arms. You remember Nora, right? She's the one who adopted Katrina rescue Phyllis a month before she was getting married, and then Phyllis and Nora's other dog trashed the house while she and her fiancé went out to dinner.

Well, Nora saw a Facebook video of a Boston terrier that Danny and Ron's director of marketing and matchmaking, Kim Tudor, had posted. "She reminded me so much of a dog named

Maxine I once had that was really special," Nora says. "I immediately started crying when I saw the video. It was just kind of visceral. Maxine had already been gone for more than ten years, but I knew I had to have this dog. I didn't understand why anybody would want to give her up."

Maisy Daisy had been found and picked up by a shelter as an unspayed stray. But she turned out to be microchipped, and when the shelter contacted her owners, they said they did not want to pay the $250 fine to retrieve her. Danny and Ron held on to her for a full week—the length of time the owners had to change their minds. But they did not relent. Unfortunately, by the time Nora saw her online and contacted them, Kim told her she had already been promised to someone else. "I was kind of heartbroken but let it go," Nora says. "What choice did I have?

"But then that adoption fell through, and Kim said that if I still wanted her—

"In my mind I was already figuring out how I would be able to get her to my house in Seattle before Kim could even finish her sentence. The answer came in the fact that Ron was planning on making a visit to Chicago to see his mother. I would fly in from Seattle and he from South Carolina, and we would rendezvous at O'Hare Airport."

Which is exactly what happened. Says Nora, "Maisy Daisy went from Ron's arms to mine as if it were the most normal thing in the world. It was like she was waiting for me."

Once Maisy Daisy arrived at her new home, Nora learned that she was "a giant bundle of love," as she calls her. "If my husband, Morgan, and I sit down on the couch to watch a TV show at the end of the day," Nora says, "she'll snuggle up next to him, lean back, and lick his face excessively. Finally, when he can't take the licking anymore, she'll lie next to him with her head cradled in his shoulder and just look at him.

"But at the same time she's like a monkey—all muscle. She has no idea how strong she is. Every day when you take her out on her leash, she runs until she hits the end of the line. As gentle and loving as she is, she's just kind of nonstop."

Nora's other four dogs don't seem to mind Maisy Daisy's turbo-charged energy, including Phyllis, the last of the Katrina dogs to still be alive, as far as we know. (We lost our own Daisy, along with Milly, a few years ago.) An old lady now, Phyllis mostly ignores Maisy Daisy, as does Bugsy, a muggle (miniature pinscher/pug cross) that Nora adopted from us as well. Hubert, a schnauzer/terrier mix and the only dog that Nora did not adopt from our rescue—"He's from Seattle Humane," she says—doesn't like all dogs and will sometimes pick on them, but he pretty much leaves Maisy Daisy alone. That said, she is not allowed to grab a toy without Hubert's approval. She accepts that he is her boss.

But Chico is *Hubert's* boss, and Maisy Daisy knows not to get in his face. He, too, traveled across country to take up residence at Nora's. Adopting him hadn't been in the plans.

"Danny was judging a horse show in Seattle," Nora says, "and one morning I brought Phyllis and Bugsy so they could say hi to him. I was curious to see if they'd remember him. It had been so many years. But the minute they heard his voice they went crazy. It was so cute, and he loved seeing them and holding them again.

"Then, out of nowhere, my daughter Lil—she was five at the time—piped up that she wanted a teacup Chihuahua. Well, of course Danny immediately started scrolling through his phone to see what teacup Chihuahuas he and Ron might have. And don't you know, Chico was available.

"Later that year, we went to the Capital Horse Challenge Show in Maryland, and Chico was shipped up there from South Carolina with some horses so we would be able to take him back to Seattle with us. He sat in the cab in the front of the truck while the horses rode behind in their trailer. He was eight at the time. I've reached the point where I would rather adopt an older dog than a puppy. One reason is that the public always wants young dogs, and I worry that older dogs get passed over too often. But also, I *like* older dogs. Already trained, they're less work. And they're soulful. I think an older dog figures it out faster that he has been rescued, and maybe that strengthens the bond.

"The first night in Maryland," Nora continues, "we took Chico back to the hotel with us with strict heartworm instructions from Danny and Ron: 'He is still being treated. Don't let him get too much exercise.' I figured, how much exercise does a teacup Chihuahua get? But the little squirrel-colored dog immediately started whipping doughnuts, running around the hotel room. It was so funny even though he wasn't supposed to be exerting himself. He's still that way at bedtime. He gets the zoomies. You try to pick him up, and he dodges you. He's a very low-energy dog in general, so it's amusing to watch.

"He also has a quirk in that he won't walk on a collar and leash. He just sits down belligerently if you try to take him out that way—it's insulting to him. So you have to take off the collar. He is willing to follow behind you but will not be tethered. He essentially does all of his business in the yard, where he also loves to climb into the wine rack and sun himself, looking for all the world like a little misshapen bottle of wine.

"Maisy Daisy wouldn't dare try to cross him. Eight-pound Chico runs the house. He used to be so mean to Bugsy," Nora says. "He'd go *'grrrr'* when Bugsy passed, just to let him know who was boss."

Things have less of a hierarchical feel between the dogs at Ylva and Jeff's house, where Cookie finally arrived around two in the morning after being stranded in North Carolina. It was already five o'clock in the morning eastern time for jet-lagged Danny. He and Cookie had to wait eight hours in the Charlotte airport for the next flight out to Southern California, and then make their way to Danny's hotel in San Juan Capistrano, where Ylva and Jeff were waiting in the deserted lobby. "Danny was more upset about the ordeal for Cookie's sake than for his own," Ylva says.

But Cookie took the travel like a trooper and was essentially no worse for the experience. "She sat in my lap for the forty-five-minute ride from the hotel to the house," Ylva explains. "I had biscuits with me to help keep her calm, but she wasn't shaking or anything. She did seem a little shy and maybe a little scared, but mostly she just looked around: 'Where am I? What's going on here?'"

Once they arrived back at the house, the other two dogs—red-haired Fergie and a Welsh corgi named Duke—accepted her right away, although Duke at first shared his human family a little begrudgingly. "When we would go to pay attention to Cookie," Ylva says, "Duke would push his way in: 'Pet *me,* pet *me!*'" He was never aggressive with Cookie, though, and eventually made full peace with her being there.

Fergie adopted Cookie as her own immediately and forever. Six years old when the new dog arrived, she would clean Cookie's eyes and ears every day. She thought Cookie was her puppy. "Fergie was one of those angel mother figures," Jeff says.

When it came to people, Cookie generally remained a little standoffish at first. "I think somebody mistreated her," Jeff comments. "We don't know what her life was like before, but we have a feeling she wasn't treated very well. If you even just waved your hands near her head while talking, she would cringe. She was very affectionate, so loving and sweet—even with newcomers after five minutes—but she had a kind of anxiety about her."

As Cookie began to settle in and approach her full size, she would go to rub her face and nose on the couch, on the bed. But it wasn't a sign of contentment, or a cute affectation. "I looked at her lips," Ylva says, "and she had blood that she was trying to wipe off. And scabs. She also had a lot of wrinkles on her lower lip and nose, like there was too much skin there. Food and things would get stuck in the crevices. I took her to the vet, and he prescribed a cream we had to apply so that the lips wouldn't keep getting inflamed." But it wasn't really working.

"'Do you think you could give her a face-lift?' I asked at the vet's office," Ylva recounts. "They thought that was a great idea." It's the kind of operation that usually a dog like a shar pei might get because all the wrinkles make that breed so itchy and uncomfortable. But Cookie happened to have this unusual anatomy.

After she came home from the face-lift, she did better but was still rubbing her nose a lot. "I didn't want her to suffer; she was still itching," Ylva says. So she and Jeff brought her in for a second nip and tuck, and she never rubbed her nose again. "We always joke about her being the only dog in the country that has had two face-lifts," Jeff says.

It was soon time for Cookie's first horse show. Ylva and Jeff don't like to leave the dogs home with a sitter when they're on the road. She did absolutely fine, hanging out with Fergie and Duke in a fenced pen that the couple had set up. But when it came time to head home a couple of days later and Ylva was packing up the trailer, Cookie jumped over the fence and into the vehicle.

"I put her back into the pen and continued packing," Ylva says, "but she jumped out like popcorn again and back into the trailer."

Jeff explains, "She panicked. She worried that she was being left again. We don't forgive those people for what they did. There's no reason any human being would want to abandon a dog like that in a home, even in a foreclosure. They could have taken her to an animal rescue organization or a local shelter."

Over time, Cookie calmed down and learned to trust her new life without reserve. Ylva and Jeff lived in a house one block from a beach just for neighborhood residents, "and because it was private," Ylva says, "dogs didn't have to be on leashes there. Cookie would go swimming with Fergie and Duke two or three times a week."

"Her first day at the beach she was insecure," Jeff says. "We have a picture of her with her legs on Ylva." But over time, she began to enjoy the water and the freedom the beach afforded her.

Cookie did become very depressed when Fergie died at the age of seventeen, after they had been together more than ten years. "We were really worried about her," Jeff says. "But a while after Fergie's death more of her personality came out, and we started to see that she became much more animated than she used to be. She took over the role of the 'big' dog, and she's much livelier now."

She has remained very sweet, though. "We used to have a cat who died when she was eighteen," Ylva says, "and she was not friendly to people. But she *loved* Cookie. Cookie would let her do anything. She would go under Cookie's chin and rub on her. We have since learned the cat was bunting. Felines have scent glands on their chins, and rubbing like that, bunting, was her way of claiming Cookie as her own: 'We share the same scent now. You are mine. We belong together.'"

Cookie is also very patient and loving toward children. Jeff says, "My daughter took in two foster children during the COVID pandemic—two sisters ages seven and three—that she went on to adopt. And then she became pregnant and had a baby boy. And Cookie is very good with all three of them." Adds Ylva, "She lets the girls kiss and pet her and is very sweet to them."

But perhaps the thing Ylva and Jeff most love about Cookie is her joy—her joy simply to be alive and to be loved. "Every time she gets up in the morning she scratches and rolls and makes happy sounds on the bed," Jeff says. "And she engages in the same ritual every night, scratching and rubbing and rolling around. It's her signal that she's good with her life. She's saying her prayers."

Ylva agrees: "She thanks God when she wakes up in the morning and then right before bed at night. Dig dig dig, rub rub rub, pray pray pray, every day of her life. It makes us feel good, because we know she's happy."

"We're kind of jealous that we're not the same way she is," Jeff says, "so appreciative of life. We human beings take a lot of stuff for granted. But I'm always relating to Cookie a little bit because she knows something I don't. She's thankful each day that she's here and that we're all together—none of that BS that people get into."

Ron, despite his initial misgivings about letting Cookie go, is glad that he made the right decision. She is so much Ylva's dog, in fact, that her hair has actually turned from auburn to blond over the years—like her Swedish "mother's" locks.

Better still, Ron gets to see Cookie every year. Ylva and Jeff drive annually to Wellington from California for the Winter Equestrian Festival and take her along. "Twelve years old now, she falls asleep in the car and wakes up to go pee," Jeff says. "She's just the greatest dog."

"She stays up in the announcer's booth with Jeff," Danny explains, "and hangs out while his voice booms over the loudspeaker: 'Now in the ring is entry number 429. This horse's name is Beyond. It's owned by So-and-So and ridden by So-and-So.' She can't really hear him anymore—Cookie has become pretty profoundly deaf in her old age—but she's happy to snuggle with Jeff, and another announcer who sits up in the booth with them adores Cookie, so she gets plenty of attention while he's working."

"She's plugging along, still going strong," Ron says, happy, and even to this day relieved for where she ended up after her rough start in life.

Admittedly, it doesn't end up right every single time. We learned that one dog we adopted out to a family up north had been given away by his owners when they decided things weren't working out. That's not allowed. It says specifically in our adoption papers that if you don't want to hold on to a dog you adopt from us, it must come back to us. We don't want to risk one of our dogs being rehomed into a situation that is not right for them; we take very special care in vetting people before they take one of our animals. The fit has to be right. Some dogs don't get on with children; some are very much house pets, when a family wants an active dog who will go hiking with them; some need a fenced-in yard; and so on. We are happy to pick up a dog at our own expense if an owner decides that for whatever reason the pet does not belong with them—no matter how many years have gone by.

However, the owners of this dog—Cyrano, a dachshund/ Chihuahua mix—dropped him off at a shelter with a high euthanasia rate. The shelter contacted us because we microchip every Danny & Ron dog, and the chip remains in our name for the length of the dog's life. We were able to get hold of a friend in a nearby city who was willing to drive down to the shelter to pick up Cyrano. But the shelter director then called us to say he was no longer ours but theirs.

Because our adoption contract includes a clause stipulating that giving up a dog to anyone but us comes with a five-thousand-dollar fine, we were able to put a lien on the house of the people who relinquished him. It is that important to us that a dog we have rescued never again ends up in a shelter.

In Cyrano's case, we also were able to involve the local police, who went to the shelter to get him for us but learned that he had "mysteriously" disappeared. In the meantime, our marketing director, Kim, found out that the shelter director was being charged with several counts of animal cruelty.

It took us two months to finally track Cyrano down, largely with the help of the police officers. They kept asking questions of shelter employees and were finally able to tie the pieces together. The dog had been ditched with some people in the area who were hiding him. Once he was found, we got him back and were able to rehome him with a loving family.

It was quite a scare. But that's truly the exception rather than the rule. In almost every single instance, when one of our dogs travels a long distance to unite with a new family, things work out splendidly, as they did for Cookie, Maisy Daisy, and Chico.

That's what keeps us willing to send dogs across the country and willing to take them ourselves if we have to. It means good things are in store for them.

Up until a few years ago, we believed all that travel would always be simply about delivering dogs to their new homes, or removing them from a home in the exceedingly rare instance that it was necessary. But more recently, there arose yet another reason we began crisscrossing the country on the dogs' behalf—one we couldn't have imagined in a million years.

Ylva Aberg laid claim to Cookie the moment she saw her picture.

Nora Thomas and her new dog Maisy Daisy at O'Hare Airport. Ron flew up from South Carolina, and Nora from Seattle, for the handoff.

Chapter 12

A Turn of Events

One January, when we were down in Florida, a man named Ron Davis came to see us at our Wellington home about adopting a companion for his Jack Russell mix, CeeCee. We had never heard of him, but being a horseman, he mingled in the same circles we did and people suggested he try our rescue.

Davis hadn't been aware of us, either, at least not in terms of our mission with dogs. But, he says, "Having been in the equestrian world—I used to ride years ago—I knew who Danny Robertshaw was because he was famous. He was one of the best hunter/jumper riders in the country."

"Danny is what Michael Phelps is to swimming or what Tom Brady is to football," Ron says proudly.

Davis was hoping for another Jack Russell–like dog. But things didn't go as he expected.

"Danny and Ron showed me around," he says. "They had a number of dogs in the house at the time and asked me a bunch of questions about what I was looking for personality-wise. I wanted something that was cuddly, that was going to get along with other dogs, with other people. I wanted something really sweet, not like a hunting dog or another breed that was really hyper. They pointed to this little Chihuahua.

"It was Little Guy," Ron says, "a tiny, fragile dog we knew would be perfect for Davis and his other pet. But he had no interest."

"'Yuck,' I thought," Davis relates. "I did not want a Chihuahua. I had such horrible ideas of what a Chihuahua was like— mean, maybe a biter. But I did find Danny and Ron interesting."

While Davis was at the Wellington house, he asked us a lot of questions. We explained to him about how we run the rescue without ever charging an adoption fee, how some seventy to one hundred dogs live in the South Carolina house at any one time and how we had to take up all the wooden floors and rugs and put down stone floors so dogs who haven't yet gotten the hang of going potty outside don't destroy the place. We told him how a phone conversation never occurs without a dog piping up in the background; how no dog who comes to us is ever euthanized because of a lack of resources; how each dog lives with us as family until someone comes to take the animal home.

He was truly interested to hear, but it was also a bit of a ruse on our part. Davis had brought CeeCee with him, and as the three of us conversed she and Little Guy started tumbling around the living room together and then chasing each other to different parts of the house, happily panting right next to each other when they needed a break.

We talked for quite a while, and by the end of the visit, we suggested to Davis that he at least take Little Guy home and try things out. If it didn't work out, we told him, he could bring him back. We truly never want a dog living where it doesn't belong.

We managed to convince him, and he left convinced of something else that day as well. "Gentlemen," he told us, "you two are going to be the subjects of my next documentary."

It turned out that Ron Davis is an award-winning filmmaker who owns a company called Docutainment. He makes movies with heavy topics, such as a Miss USA Pageant contestant with cerebral palsy; an Amish plow horse that was rescued from the glue factory and in Seabiscuit fashion became a national show jumping champion; a transgender woman who married a Black man in the Deep South almost fifty years ago.

"We just kind of chuckled about it when he made his declaration," Danny says, "and looked at him like he was crazy. We figured, what is he going to film us doing? Feeding the dogs every morning and picking up poop?"

"They told me they were boring," Davis says. "But I instinctively knew they were interesting. I knew they had big hearts. And I knew that anybody who does something like what they did had to have interesting stories. *Everyone's* interesting, but these guys were wearing it on their sleeve."

After he left, we didn't give it another thought. But about a week later he began calling. "I was still finishing up another film," Davis says, "but I started wooing them, taking them to dinner, trying to get them to agree to it."

We kept telling him we weren't interested. Part of it was that we had no idea a documentary could be entertaining. "In our minds," Danny says, "it was like being forced to watch the evening news when you're twelve. Who wants to watch a movie where we say you have to make sure a dog doesn't have worms? How could that be interesting to anyone with all the other more glamorous and exciting choices out there?"

Plus, we really didn't see our story as having any dramatic tension. We were just people who loved dogs and officially developed into a rescue in order to be able to raise funds to help the animals we cared about.

We were afraid of the invasion into our lives, too. What if we said the wrong thing? What if the film didn't come out right? It added up to a fear of failure—letting someone go ahead and do all the work and then watching it bomb, or worse, somehow hurting the dogs' cause. As it was, we struggled with funds, and literally couldn't afford to come off wrong. As much as the rescue had moved forward over the years—Lyle Lovett even came to judge one of our Lip Sync events—the cost of the dogs' needs always outpaced the influx of donations.

Davis understood. "You lose control of your life to an extent, and how it's portrayed," he says. But he kept at it. "Danny and Ron didn't really give me hard nos," he explains. "They just kept saying they didn't find themselves interesting."

He did finally convince us, or maybe just wore us down after many months, and then it was quite a while until filming began, because he was finishing up another movie.

We really didn't know what we were in for. But we soon learned that it was not necessarily going to be easy. Says Ron, "When the camera started rolling and Davis asked, 'What was your first

Christmas like without your parents after they disowned you?' I immediately started crying."

Similarly, Danny comments that when he was asked to talk about his relationship with his father he found it very difficult. "Ron and I would both come away sometimes mentally and physically drained," he says.

Ron echoes Danny almost exactly. "We were just being ourselves—it wasn't like we were actors playing a role—but when you start digging into old things, and getting into the family stuff, it becomes emotionally draining. We felt whipped because he pulled out so many dark places in our lives—he had us pull them out and expose them. A lot of times it makes you feel that pain again."

"Stuff that was buried had to be put into words," Danny adds. "You go to bed every night with a ton of feelings, but you don't always go to bed *saying* your feelings. They're always there, but they had been put to rest, and now they had to be reawakened."

We felt guilty, too. "Sometimes," Danny says, "you can be saying the truth of how stuff is, or how it was, but you still don't like how it sounds when you hear the words come out. For instance, in situations with my dad and about growing up, and about my mom and her alcoholism, talking about some of that, I feared it sounded harsh, or judgmental. In the end they're gone, and I didn't want it to seem like I was bad-mouthing these people I loved so much. But to get the truth of it, you have to say certain things and go to things you might have kept hidden and get yourself to an okay place about it. Still, to talk it out and go through it again and not know what you sound like—and not even know whether it's going to make the final cut in the movie—is not fun."

Ron felt the same way. "My biggest fear was being totally honest," he says. "It was very hard talking about being disowned and not wanting to come across like I was speaking against my parents. It was what it was—their refusing to talk to me for seven years happened, and at a time that I was really suffering—and I was very honest about it right up front in the filming. But I had been able to build back a relationship with my parents. And my mother was still alive, and I had a wonderful rapport with her. With the little bit of time she had left—she was close to ninety by that point—I did not want to damage our closeness or to hurt her in any way. It wasn't that I didn't want to answer Davis's questions. I just didn't want to stir up old wounds or watch her have to see things in her last days that would have made her uncomfortable. I think Mom knew I was gay, for instance, but it was just never discussed. Making it harder still was that Davis even went up to Chicago to interview Mom. That part didn't make it into the film, but it made uncomfortable realities feel that much closer."

Another thing that was hard was that we could never figure out how Davis would put together all the pieces he was filming in order to have a *story*. He filmed us here, there, and everywhere, he and his crew following us from horse show to horse show and from dog emergency to dog emergency, including during weather crises out of state where dogs' and people's lives were overturned. How was it all going to come together, we wondered? It's not like he was showing us what he was doing as he went along. Things felt . . . not so much out of sequence as *un*sequenced. It was unnerving not to know how events were going to be put together, what was going to be cut and what was going to stay in and what was going to be spliced with what. Out of literally hundreds of hours of filming, no more than ninety minutes were going to make it into the film.

Then, too, while he spent a lot of time speaking to the two of us together, he also spent many hours with each of us alone. And while we have no secrets with each other, it added to our sense of disorientation. What might Ron say that Danny had never heard before? Or what might Danny say in a way that Ron had never really heard, or completely understood?

But for all of our angst, there were lots of interesting and downright delightful and funny moments, too—a number of them involving the dogs. Most of the time the dogs were just supposed to do whatever they wanted and be filmed in the act. But there were times that Davis and his cameraman, Clay Westervelt, wanted to capture certain occurrences. For instance, they wanted to get footage of the dogs running outside through the doggie door, which often happens when we finish feeding. A bunch of them stampede through at once.

The first time they tried to film it, it was a fiasco. The dogs jumped off the side of the little ramp that we had set up for them instead of going forward onto the grass—and then licked the camera lens, which was low to the ground, or Clay's face, all excited as they were about somebody new being out there with them. The dogs who felt spooked by newcomers, on the other hand, ran off to the side and wouldn't come anywhere near him. We thought we had it all staged for the moment and that it would be so easy. After all, running through the doggie door was something the dogs did lots of times throughout each day. But the novelty of the situation threw them off. And it's not like you can keep bringing in the dogs and sending them back out again. They don't understand "takes."

Davis would have to come up with another plan for moments like those, like filming from farther away. He did get great footage, but it took a while.

The dogs created other artistic challenges, too, but Davis and Clay were always up to the task. In fact, one of the most enlightening things about going from never having even been on a film set to becoming the subject of a film was learning how much art goes into making a movie. For instance, anytime Clay filmed a dog, he always did it at dog level. When Davis was focused on us, however, Clay always had the camera on his shoulder.

Clay even made a gadget with a camera on it. He mounted it on skateboard wheels and would run it across the floor on a little train track type of thing. That way, if a dog was lying down, the camera could come right by, film the animal, and then go on to the next dog. Clay wasn't just a cameraman. Like Davis, he was truly an artist, and his and Davis's artistry showed again and again.

In one scene, at a dog shelter in Louisiana, a dragonfly on a post all of a sudden took off and flew free. We're not sure if that was caught on purpose, but it was so clever in the editing. Here we were taking all these dogs from the shelter and now they, too, were going to fly free.

Even the way they filmed the flowers at the doghouse was affecting. We will often spread the ashes of dogs who have left this life in a garden of lilies and irises we created for that purpose. Lilies symbolize that the soul has departed. And in Greek mythology, the Greek goddess Iris acted as the link between heaven and earth. She was, in fact, the personification of the rainbow—perfect, because dogs who move on are said to cross the Rainbow Bridge. The iris also represents faith and hope for a better tomorrow, which we need when we have to say goodbye to a dog we love.

Well, Davis and Clay came at dawn a number of times to capture the irises with the morning dew dripping off them as the sun broke. We believe they were trying to make the point that even as we lose those we love, a new day comes—a day filled with beauty—and we find something poignant in our grieving that enables us to keep going. As for the lilies, Davis wanted our hands to be closer to their blooms—and changed the shot several times to elicit just the visual effect he was going for. Nothing was random other than some of the antics of the dogs.

The way they filmed euthanized dogs being taken from a shelter in large plastic bags and then thrown into a ditch gave that scene special meaning, too. It reminded us of the scene in *Dead Man Walking* when the Sean Penn character must face execution for having murdered a young couple. As he meets his end, the earth is shown from above in all its splendor—the trees, the landscape. But the dead couple is a stain on the beauty—it can't be removed, and that will remain as his legacy in perpetuity.

Davis and Clay filmed the killed dogs the same way—from above. It brought into high relief what it means to put down so many innocent dogs whose only crime was having been born and then unloved.

Along with filming so artistically, Davis gave us rules. "From day one," Ron says, "he instructed us not to even start to talk about anything to him when we were not filming. 'I want to hear everything for the first time in front of the camera,' he said. 'It has to be *bang*, fresh.'"

Adds Danny, "He also didn't want us to rehearse how we'd respond to anything."

"And when he was filming, he would often put two fingers on his eyes," Ron comments. "Being new to this, we kind of naturally wanted to look at the camera while talking—it looks like a big eye in itself, and you figure you're supposed to be looking straight into the lens. But that's not the way it works with camera angles. We needed to be looking at *him*. It would get so comical at times. We'd break out laughing and have to reshoot.

"You also couldn't be whimsical with your answers," Ron explains. "He wanted answers to the specific questions he asked us—not less, not more."

"It was brutal," says Danny in a joking manner, conceding that he tends to respond to questions in a kind of circular fashion. A common exchange when you're talking with Danny, in fact, is "Yeah, but what about. . . ." With him responding, "I'm getting to that."

"Davis was a hard taskmaster," Danny says, smiling. "And when he asked us questions, we couldn't just start out with the answer. We had to repeat part of the question to keep us grounded and to keep the viewer in the loop. It helped me from straying off the path as much as I would ordinarily."

As things were beginning to come together and they had begun the editing process, Davis and Clay wanted to retake certain scenes. We'd have to look and make sure we could find the same clothes we had on the day we first did the scene. We needed to make sure the room looked the same. Davis didn't want anything like the moment *The Wizard of Oz's* Dorothy pelts the trees with apples while wearing plain black shoes instead of the iconic ruby slippers she had on a couple of seconds earlier, or the scene in *Pretty Woman* where Julia Roberts is eating a croissant, until the camera goes to Richard Gere for a minute and then comes back to her eating a pancake.

Finally, after about a year of filming on and off and then another eight months or so for editing, the movie was where Davis wanted it to be, and it was time to premiere it. But he wanted us to view it by ourselves first. "You can see yourself in a little video and not be taken aback," he told us, "but to see yourself on a massive screen is much different." He wanted us to be able to react in private before the film went public. He rented an entire movie theater to screen it just for the two of us, for which we were very thankful.

And react we did. "For me it was *really* emotional watching it," Ron says. "They created a score and had an orchestra play the music, and to see ourselves and the music and everything come together, I felt overwhelmed. I cried many times."

Danny felt the same way, and talks about moments in the film he could not have known about in advance. "Hearing Ron say what he was feeling when I was not expected to live—" he comments before trailing off. "We had talked so many times about the what-ifs and about our feelings for each other, but it stirred so much emotion in me to hear him express his emotions when I was not with him, and made me understand even better what he had gone through and the meaning of our relationship."

Ron, for his part, hadn't previously known what Danny said about his own father and his family for the film, and that, too, connected us to each other all the more.

We also loved the title: *Life in the Doghouse.* We always refer to our home as the doghouse and say that the dogs let us live there with them, and we got a kick out of Davis riffing off that.

Of course, we loved the film for its own sake as well and believed it shed the best light on the rescue and what unwanted dogs go through, how vulnerable their lives are. We were thrilled about that because it was the reason we finally consented to do the movie in the first place. We thought if we could draw attention to homeless dogs' plight, it might serve to get more people involved.

But still, we had no idea how anybody else would react. It's one thing to be enamored of a film that features you. How others would take it in remained an open question. We would learn very soon.

The film premiered in Wellington the very next night, Friday,

April 6, 2018. We had several family members fly down for the debut—Ron's sister and Danny's nieces and nephews. We both had butterflies in our stomachs to the max.

On one hand, we needn't have been anxious. The eight hundred people in attendance gave us a standing ovation, and we were thrilled. On the other hand, we couldn't help but wonder if it was because many of them knew us or knew *of* us by dint of being in the horse show world. But the way they received the movie turned out not to be a fluke.

Life in the Doghouse was featured at film festivals all over the country and received rave reviews. We were zigzagging across the United States to thunderous applause and heartfelt approval. Davis's work was a success. It won Best Documentary at the Tryon International Film Festival and was chosen as an Official Selection at the Frameline Film Festival in San Francisco, the Newport Film Festival in Rhode Island, and the Provincetown Film Festival on Cape Cod. At the Provincetown festival, an old friend of Danny's did not stand up to clap with everyone else when the credits rolled. "I thought he had fallen asleep," Danny says, "and went to rouse him. But he was awake. 'I'm just so overwhelmed,' the friend said. 'I can't even get up. I've known you most of my life, and yet I haven't known you at all.'"

"The Provincetown organizers said to us that they hardly ever get standing ovations for movies the way ours did," Ron notes. "And people were just so kind to us everywhere. Every time we walked down the street in Provincetown once the film was shown, people would say, 'Oh my God, you're the dog guys. We just want to meet you.'

"We had a similar reaction in Rhode Island. The Newport Film Festival takes place on a large polo field, and there are always at least a thousand people there watching. The evening *Life in the Doghouse* played, the people who were running the festival told us that usually ten minutes before the end of the movie, people run to their cars because there's only one driveway out and they don't want to get stuck in line. But not that night," Ron says. "We didn't leave until midnight. The line was so long just shaking people's hands, meeting viewers. I mean, it was really touching."

The film festivals even garnered us some significant national publicity. We were interviewed on the *Today* show and were written up in big-city newspapers including the *Chicago Tribune* and *The Boston Globe*.

Besides the headiness of the acclaim, watching the documentary so many times in different cities gave us a renewed understanding of ourselves. "There's a point in the movie where I say something about not understanding how people could just abandon their dogs," Ron says, "and then it shifts immediately to me talking about how my parents abandoned me. I must have watched the film seventeen times before I made the connection and understood the point Davis had made in his editing. It hit me like a ton of bricks, and I guess I now had knowledge of myself and what drove me that I had never quite had on a conscious level."

"It added to all the ways the movie had a tremendous impact on our lives," Danny says.

And then our fifteen minutes of fame were up. Or so we thought. The film festivals came to their natural close, and Davis ended up selling the movie rights to a company called FilmRise, a motion picture distribution outfit. We kind of put the whole thing on an emotional shelf, so to speak. Then, on June 1, 2019, *Life in the Doghouse* premiered on Netflix.

The ground literally shifted beneath our feet. Our website

crashed immediately; we had to put up thirteen new servers to handle all the traffic. And we needed to hire three people just to answer the three hundred to six hundred e-mails that were now coming in daily, not just from the United States and Europe but from all over the world—Australia, the Philippines, South Korea, and many other countries. We also had to ramp up on Facebook after having gained ten thousand new followers within the space of a few weeks.

Ellen DeGeneres tweeted at us later that month: "I just watched 'Life in the Doghouse' on Netflix. What this couple has done for rescue dogs is incredible. Go watch it, and then if you're like me, you're gonna wanna support them."

We also received social media shout-outs from celebrities including Mary-Kate Olsen, Nickelback, and Mike Bloomberg's daughter Georgina Bloomberg, a noted animal welfare advocate. We were even invited on various news and entertainment shows—with people who adopted dogs we rescued writing to let us know that their pets had come running to the television when they heard our voices!

What took us by surprise even more than any of that is that people were recognizing us as we went about our lives. We would get stopped in airports. "I saw your movie! Would you sign my boarding pass? Can we take a picture?"

"I even had a lady recognize me in Lowe's who asked me to sign her receipt," Ron says, "and then the cashier goes, 'I know you, too.'"

"We went to New York for our anniversary that year to see more plays," Danny relates, "and got stopped so many times on the street, in restaurants. We were blown away by how many people knew who we were. When we were leaving a theater after seeing *The Lion King,* a little boy behind us on a series of escalators we needed to take to reach street level kept staring at us.

We didn't know what was going on. We thought maybe it was because Ron is so tall and towers above everyone else.

"The dad kept saying to his son, 'Leave them alone. Don't do that.' Finally, the father turned to us and said, 'My son is so excited because you are the guys from *Life in the Doghouse*. We didn't want to bother you.'"

It was no bother! It was exciting and kind of wondrous, and we kept thinking that as pleased as people seemed to be to spot us, we had been able to send a message to so many about rescue dogs and their need for homes.

Terrific things happened closer to home, too. For one, we developed a great rapport with Ron Davis. He did us such a good turn and even pledged his net proceeds from *Life in the Doghouse* to Danny & Ron's Rescue. He is a really good person besides being an incredible filmmaker.

Davis boomerangs the sentiment right back. "The guys were not only fun and agreeable," he says. "They were really available and willing to go out on a limb, whether emotionally or with their schedule. They were very accommodating to the process." Even more important, Davis says, "I think they're the two most selfless people I've ever met, for sure, and not just because of the dogs but because of everything they do for *people*—and they do it no matter what they're going through. Danny was in excruciating pain a couple of years ago—something was pressing on a nerve in his neck, almost to the point that he became paralyzed by it. But still he dressed up as Santa to fulfill children's wish lists at the Christmas party for the Caridad Center, one of the largest free health-care clinics in the country. They provide medical and dental care for uninsured and underserved children in Florida's Palm Beach County. And Ron has horrible pain in his hand joints because of rheumatoid arthritis—he has been on all kinds of medications for it—yet is always about other people. They never stop, even when their lives are not so great. They're involved in so many different things.

"One day we were filming at a shelter," Davis continues, "and this woman came in with a cat that she found on the street. It was a mess, with some kind of awful gook coming out of its eyes. She was just dropping it off, but Ron told her, 'If you adopt this cat and give it a good home, we'll take care of all of its food and medical expenses for the rest of its life.' And she did. They literally saved that cat's life on the spot.

"And they'll go out in the woods and trap wounded animals to tend to them. They're very hands on with all of it. There was some terrible flooding from a storm in Baton Rouge during the time I was filming, and down they went. It was hot and sweaty, and they were delivering food and medicine for people's dogs—not sending other people to do it for them. And most people, they go to help in a crisis and then when they are no longer needed for that emergency, go back to their regular lives. But they were *looking* for ways to help once they had become involved in Katrina. They were not waiting for emergencies to be dropped off at their doorstep. And this is *on top of* having a full-time career."

The camaraderie has extended to the dogs, we are happy to report. The good feeling we observed between Little Guy and Ron Davis's dog CeeCee was not just about their being new to each other. Once Davis took them home, they got along famously—and do to this day. "They cuddle and sleep together," Davis says, providing just the company for each other that he had been hoping for.

In fact, the two dogs got on so well from the beginning that the first week Davis started filming us he adopted Mr. Brown, another dog at the house who really needed a home of his own. "They had seventy-five or so dogs in the house that first week," Davis says. "It's kind of surprising when you walk in for the first time—but the little, solid brown dachshund mix just stood out. I have no idea why he made more of an impression than the others. Why, when you look across a crowded room, are you attracted to someone and not someone else? Maybe it's because his tail was wagging a million miles an hour.

"I started fostering him at first," Davis says. "I'd take him back to the hotel with me at night. Then, when we had completed filming for that week, I was supposed to fly home from South Carolina to Florida. But I rented a car so I could drive Mr. Brown back to the house.

"CeeCee took to him right away, but Little Guy needed some time. Other than CeeCee, Little Guy hasn't been the friendliest with new dogs. And Mr. Brown, for his part, is not a dog dog. He really prefers people."

The two mighty males, one twelve pounds and the other sixteen, did eventually make their peace with each other, but Mr. Brown doesn't cuddle with and sleep together with the other three dogs. Yes, the other *three*. Davis ended up taking in a fourth dog named Bentley. "My niece had adopted him from a rescue on Florida's west coast," he says, "but she could no longer take care of him. She has two kids and he was getting neglected. So I took him." So much for having an aversion to Chihuahuas. Bentley is the same breed as Little Guy.

We are thrilled that Davis gave Bentley a better life. "We don't care where a rescue comes from," Danny says. "We just want the rescuing to keep happening."

Of course, with the popularity of the movie—it was streamed more than three million times around the world—we received many more inquiries about adopting a "Danny & Ron dog" and were able to start moving more of them out of the doghouse and into people's families.

By that point we had plenty of adopters outside the horse community, but now, from across the country, and even internationally, people were looking up our dogs on Facebook to see which might be right for them. And donations started coming in from as far away as South Korea. We had to begin calculating currencies on the foreign exchange market.

We were on the way, we realized, to being able to expand our outreach that much further. Animals in all kinds of situations were going to be able to receive help that might otherwise have been unavailable to them.

On the set of *Life in the Doghouse* (our kitchen!) with filmmaker Ron Davis and cameraman Clay Westervelt.

* * *

Meersey, a five-pound Chihuahua who reminds us of a meerkat the way she sits on her hind legs, has one limb that from the knee down is turned completely backward from the way it's supposed to be facing. She was literally kicked around the house by her abusive owner with such force that he broke the bone there and dislocated it forever. Danny learned of her at Florida's Palm Beach County Animal Control. The veterinarian there said the dog would probably be euthanized because she was not really adoptable—she snarled and growled at anyone who came near her and bit them if they got close enough.

Danny asked to go back to see her, and she immediately jumped into his arms. She fell in love with Ron pretty quickly, too, but not anybody else. No one could get near her or even think about picking her up, although she was okay around other dogs. A little white Chihuahua in our care named Sweet Pea became her best friend.

We have had her about four years, affectionately coming to call her Meer Meer, and she now allows exactly three other people to hold her (it's hard for those who visit us because she's a dog you just want to scoop up). She is still very shy and frightened and can react aggressively if she feels her safety is in danger; she has been through too much.

We took her and Sweet Pea down to Wellington with us one autumn when we stayed in Florida for the Winter Equestrian Festival. Isabelle, a terrier mix, came along, too. We thought we would come back to South Carolina in March but found ourselves stranded until June because of the COVID-19 pandemic.

Everyone did fine, but we were so glad to finally be able to return home as summer drew near. The entire staff was at the house—they had put out "Welcome Home" balloons and spruced up the garden spectacularly. Two staff members came to the car, and each opened a back door from either side to help with luggage.

That's where Meer Meer was sitting. The surprise of the staff members coming near her after the long car ride from Florida combined with all the hoopla was more than she could bear. She bolted from the back seat to the front, over Danny's lap, and out the front door, which he had just opened.

Our entire thirteen-acre property at the doghouse is fenced in, but without our knowing it tiny Meer Meer was able to limbo herself under the electric gate at the lip of the driveway, which has a very narrow space at the bottom of about five inches.

Thinking Meer Meer was still somewhere on the grounds, the entire staff walked every inch of the property for several hours with no luck. We then called a company that has search-and-rescue bloodhounds. The owner of the firm instructed the hounds to sniff the bedding in the car and also to sniff Sweet Pea and Isabelle so that they knew they would be looking for the one scent that was not present—Meer Meer's. To our surprise, the bloodhounds led us down the driveway, out the front gate, to the left along the woods, then into a hayfield. From there we went to a cornfield and onto a gravel road to someone's house with old barns and other structures on the property.

Then the hounds had us traipsing through another cornfield, more hayfields, and yet another house. It was now 9:30 at night and pitch black. The search had been going on for more than six hours and had to be given up for the night.

"I did not go to sleep," Ron says. "I stayed up all night, driving up and down the roads, reeling in panic overload. Living out in the country, Meer Meer could have fallen prey to coyotes, bobcats, rattlesnakes, water snakes, moccasins, hawks, eagles, and owls. Birds of those species can easily carry away a five-pound dog."

Danny, for his part, went in and out of fitful sleep all night, tossing and turning. The two of us could hear coyotes howling in the night. Our hearts pounded.

At daybreak, we went back to the routine we had been away from for so many months, something we had been looking forward to. But we acted perfunctorily in our haste in order to return to the task of finding our missing pet. We fed all the dogs, medicated those who were taking one or another drug, and let them out and back in. "Then," says Ron, "I got in the car and started driving the roads, calling her, calling her." Danny trained show horses in the meantime; there was a lot of catching up to do given that we had been away so long.

Earlier that morning, we had asked Kim, our marketing director, to create a lost-dog poster, and she went to a UPS store to have forty printed up. We put them at every crossroad, taped them to road signs, to caution signs, wherever.

The bloodhounds came back to keep searching, and we began to tackle the area on foot. It was 95 degrees, with 100 percent humidity. We were worried to death that Meer Meer would become too thirsty and overheated.

At around one o'clock in the afternoon, the woman who lived in the house we'd passed with the bloodhounds the day before told us she saw our dog in a shaded spot right near the beginning of her driveway. Unfortunately, a farmhand on a tractor also saw Meer Meer and tried to catch her, and she ran as fast as she could down a mowed edge between a hayfield and a cornfield. You can never chase a scared dog; that will only send it farther away.

More cornfields, more hayfields, through some barbed-wire

fencing, across a little creek, and then through another field. Still no luck. The owner of the bloodhounds put a drone in the air to see if he could detect any activity in one of the cornfields—the corn was unusually high and unusually dense and impossible to navigate well at eye level. But even with the drone, nothing came into view.

There were about ten or eleven of us now on the search, and with the heat and humidity, many become dizzy and nauseated, and started to see stars. Around 8:30 that evening, as the sun was going down, someone on our staff called to say he'd seen Meer Meer running in a pasture by the old barn at the house of one of our neighbors. Danny went home and retrieved Sweet Pea and Isabelle so they could run around the barn and start barking to entice Meer Meer to come out if she was indeed in there. But it didn't work. There was no sign of her.

Then it was dark again. We put up deer cameras around the area and set up three traps with canned cat food, which has a strong scent and might have attracted her. Ron checked his pedometer—he'd tallied more than sixteen miles of walking that day in search of her, and so, more or less, had everyone else. We were all feeling literally crippled—the weather was just so hot, and we'd covered so much more ground than we expected to.

But there'd be no sleep for a second night in a row. "Around midnight," Ron says, " I was walking around the yard, calling for her, thinking that maybe in the silence of the darkness, without any cars driving down the road, she'd hear my voice from the woods and come running. The moon was waxing—almost full—which gave me hope.

"But then I started to hear the coyotes howl again, and the tears streamed down my cheeks, my stomach churning, my mind going to all the bad places. I started yelling for her louder and quicker, but to no avail. Finally, disheartened, I turned back toward the house. The coyotes had quieted down, but the hoot owls had started up. More stomach turning."

The next morning, Ron bought a new drone because the bloodhound owner's wasn't working well. It cost $1,700, and that was on top of $2,000 for the bloodhound service. He also bought four more deer cameras for $150 apiece because they had an app you could download to your phone that alerted you if there had been any motion.

We then bought eight more traps. The ones we have are really for big dogs, and maybe Meer Meer was too light to trigger them. We spread the traps around the area. And we took our clothes from the day before and our pillowcases from the bed and put them in various locations so Meer Meer could get a sense of us if she came across the odors.

All that day—two days after she jumped out of the car and now with all the gear in place to provide a better chance of detecting her, including more time with the bloodhounds—we did not have a single sighting.

That night, thunderstorms with drenching rain, high winds, loud booms, and lightning hit the area. Meer Meer had never fended for herself outside in her life. She went out to relieve herself—that was it.

"I was wound up tight as a tick," Ron says. "Couldn't sleep yet another night."

The woman who owned the house near where Meer Meer was first sighted called to say we could lift up floorboards in her barn to see if the little dog had hidden herself under them. We were so grateful. The next morning, around 6:15, before we and the staff headed out to keep searching, Kim sent all of us St. Anthony's prayer and told us to say it out loud; St. Anthony is the patron saint of lost things.

> *... I turn to you today with childlike love and deep con-*
> *fidence.*
> *You have helped countless children of God*
> *to find the things they have lost.*
> *Material things, and more importantly,*
> *the things of the spirit: faith, hope, and love.*
> *... I come to you with confidence;*
> *Help me in my present need ...*

Neither of us is terribly religious. Praying for the return of a lost dog is not the kind of thing we are apt to do.

Ron went and bought plastic fencing and staking posts at Lowe's to put around the barn in case Meer Meer was really there. That way, she wouldn't be able to run away.

While he was finishing up at the store, Danny's niece, Christy, who works at the rescue, called to say she could see Meer Meer going down a driveway that was about two miles in length. "I literally started driving as fast as I could," Ron says. "When I reached the spot, I could see Meer Meer's little tiny telltale hop hop hop that she has because of her busted leg, and was very cautious because I knew she might not be able to recognize me in her panicked state.

"I got out of the car and crouched down, even though she was two hundred fifty feet away. She saw me and put her chest on the ground and crawled like a cat—I knew at that point that she was not going to bolt. She was wiggling and wiggling, and when I finally reached her—walking, not running, in order not to spook her—she jumped into my arms. I started bawling immediately."

Danny was at the barn tending to the horses and equestrians. "When Ron called me," says Danny, "I started crying, too."

It had been three days of hell, but we got back a dog we know we will never be able to adopt out because of her shyness and occasional aggression. We took her home, gave her a bath, and fed her, and then she dug under the covers on our bed and stayed there from 11:30 that morning until 5:30 the next morning, when we rose to feed all the dogs.

All of us on the staff later compared notes, and it turned out every single one of us had said St. Anthony's prayer out loud. Ron said it ten times.

You have to wonder. But despite our good fortune, we didn't leave the future entirely in St. Anthony's hands. There's now a tiny piece of wire under the electric gate so that even a dog as small as Meer Meer can never get under it.

Ron holding Meer Meer as soon as she was found.

Chapter 13

Broadening Our Horizons

Maybe it was the news footage of search-and-rescue dogs rummaging through forests burning up around them to help save vulnerable animals. Maybe it was the video of the woman who took off her shirt and wrapped it around a koala trying to make his way through a raging wildfire with burn marks all over him, finally carrying him to safety in the intense heat and giving him water from a bottle while he cried. Maybe it's that koalas are about the size of a small to medium-size dog—two to two and a half feet and up to about thirty-three pounds. Whatever the reason, the same month that *Life in the Doghouse* came out, devastating bush fires began that ended up incinerating 46 million acres in Australia, and as time wore on and the flames continued to consume the forests and the animals who lived in them we knew we had to do something.

The koalas seemed particularly vulnerable to us. Harmless little animals that spend so much of their lives high up in eucalyptus trees, they were doomed by the way they live. Eucalyptus wood burns particularly quickly and intensely, and the trees have a way of being ripe for "crown fires" in their top limbs, where koalas like to be. Tens of thousands of koalas were estimated to be killed during the many months of fires, while many others were found starving and scarred, often separated from their mothers. A koala, a type of marsupial, is no bigger than a jelly bean when it's born, weighing less than a tenth of an ounce as it learns its way around its mother's pouch. The species is said by some to be sliding toward extinction, in no small part because of the fires.

"The animals looked so innocent," Ron says. "It was pathetic. Seeing footage of them with their fur burned off, their skin raw—there had to be a way to help them by assisting the search-and-rescue dogs that were locating them among the flames. It was such a horrific thing to watch on the news."

That's why we sent a donation to the Koala Hospital Conservation Fund in Australia's Port Macquarie. Because the people there were boots-on-the-ground while we were on the other side of the world, we felt they would be in the best position to know how to use the money to help the search-and-rescue dogs and their trainers or for other koala-saving purposes. We always understood that animal rescue has no borders—either between countries or between species—but receiving such an overwhelming response from people around the world after the movie about us came to the small screen drove that point home. Across the globe, we are all in it together.

We also try to help out in Aruba. Most often people think of it strictly as a Caribbean island paradise, which it most certainly is, but it's also a place dogs need help. We learned by going there on vacation that dogs in Aruba are often well loved but that funds for spay/neuter programs are lacking, as are medical supplies—everything from heartworm and flea and tick preventatives to antibiotics for treating infections. That's why we stepped up efforts to try to help out there, contributing drugs and dog food and sometimes paying veterinary bills for expensive procedures.

Danny & Ron's marketing director, Kim Tudor, interjects, "That doesn't begin to describe their involvement. During the week or two they spend in Aruba if they manage to get away in any given year, they fly down with suitcases that are filled with thousands of dollars' worth of medical supplies, including vaccines. And once they arrive, they shop locally for an Aruban dog rescue called New Life for Paws, buying hundreds and hundreds of pounds of food. On their trip home, they always return with two puppies in dire medical need—because two dogs is the maximum number they are allowed to bring on the plane. There is never a day in their life that is not about rescue, even when they try to steal away for a few days of vacation after working seven days a week all year long."

How could we not help out? The woman who runs New Life for Paws, Natalya Yermak, is much like us. She lives with sixty dogs in her own house at any one time—except without any staff to help her. She calls the animals "my babies."

She had emigrated to the United States from Ukraine and

was vacationing in Aruba when she began to learn the plight of the dogs there. "I was on vacation with five other women," she says, "and found a dog in the middle of the road. I ruined everybody's day.

"I talked somebody local into putting the dog in their car, and we drove to the veterinarian's office. 'This is a half-dead dog,' they told me. 'She is dying. She is not just heartworm positive but *super*-heartworm positive. And she is pregnant. She won't make it.'

"That same night I helped her deliver her puppies in somebody's house on a piece of plywood. She had no strength to push them out; her head was turning blue from the exertion. The next morning she died after delivering fourteen babies.

"I extended my vacation to bottle-feed all the newborns. I could see that there were so many uncared-for street dogs on the island. You start to view things with new eyes. I came home to the States but had to come back. This was ten years ago.

"Danny and Ron, they contacted me at one point and then came to visit me to see what I was doing, how I was handling things," Natalya says. "Every year, they not only bring me supplies—flea and tick medicine, deworming medicine, everything. They also help me with the vet bills. I always have enormous vet bills at different local veterinary practices—thousands and thousands of dollars. I can never catch up. When they come they pay the entire bill and knock it to zero every single year. And this is on top of their own bills they have to pay for the dogs they take care of back home.

"They also take me to buy many thousands of dollars' worth of supplies to last the entire year—pallets piled high with huge bags of food, cleaning supplies, pee pee pads, Lysol, toilet paper, laundry detergent, dishwashing liquid—anything for the dogs and to keep the place clean for them.

"And yes, every single time they come, they take two dogs from me and bring them back home with them. They always tell me, 'Give us the ones you think are least adoptable—that you will have the hardest time getting anyone to take.'"

This year we took Almond and Breeze. Almond needs an eye taken out; he was born with a congenital defect that will never allow him to see out of it and can only cause him problems down the line. And Breeze has to have surgeries on both her hind legs. She was born with deformities in the two limbs that are not allowing proper alignment of the ball-and-socket joints needed for proper mobility. The dogs will stay with us until they are rehabilitated from the surgeries and become secure living at the doghouse, after which we will let them be adopted.

"They are amazing people," Natalya says. "I fall asleep with their movie every night. It makes me feel that I am not alone. They're like my family."

Natalya was orphaned in Ukraine at the age of sixteen, when her adoptive mother, a single woman who had survived the Holocaust, died. She has no brothers or sisters or extended family. She, too, knows something about feeling abandoned. We are happy to be her family.

"I love Danny and Ron so much," Natalya says in return. "They are such a calming couple—so nice, so good. True friends. I pray for Danny to be healthy and strong. Their hearts are so kind."

We have been lucky enough to meet others along the way who are also loving, and very caring about both animals and people and so devoted to them. Among them is Elana Morgan, who heads War Dogs Making It Home, a Chicago-based organization that pairs veterans with service dogs.

"I kept reading about military veterans committing suicide," Elana says. "So many veterans have PTSD [post-traumatic stress disorder] or TBI [traumatic brain injury] because of what they have been through in combat zones, and they turn to drinking or drugs—or become homeless because they can't deal. Many end up taking their own lives. Right now there are twenty-two suicides a day. As we speak, a veteran is about to kill himself. It's both men and women.

"I know about PTSD because I was raised by people who had it. My father and my grandparents escaped Lithuania when the Russian occupation began. My father was only four, and my grandfather escaped the men's concentration camp and rescued my grandmother and my father and his siblings from where they were being housed. They finally made it to Canada after a harrowing few years hiding out in Germany and then England.

"My father, my grandparents, my aunts and uncles, all drank because of what they had been through. They didn't know the term 'PTSD,' but drinking was how they tried to deal with it.

"We also always had a lot of pets in the family. My grandfather kept boxers and Dobermans, and whenever he was stressed, he would go for a walk with the dogs and come back calmer. My father, too, as an adult had his own special dog that would just calm him.

"I think that's what gave me the idea to pair rescue dogs with veterans who have PTSD or TBI. I run a dog-training kennel and felt that with rescues we could help veterans inexpensively rather than pay many thousands of dollars for service dogs with special pedigrees.

"The dogs who come from Danny & Ron's Rescue are in better shape than the dogs who come from other rescues, and not just because all their medical needs have already been taken care of, sometimes at considerable cost—spaying and neutering, vaccines, medical care for injuries. It's also that many rescues, when they take a dog, they want to place it as soon as possible. Danny and Ron don't do it that way. The dog comes and lives with them first, gets to understand what it's like to be in a house among people. And it gives them time to understand the dog and figure out whether it will make a good service dog. They're real intuitive about it. They very much know what I need."

Says Ron, "They need to be very keen dogs, very smart, and needing a mission. They want to be busy working."

"'Keen' is a perfect word," Danny comments. "A service dog for someone with PTSD needs to be able to focus intensely. She can't be easily distracted."

"That's it," Elana says. "Danny and Ron know what I'm looking for. Also, a calm dog, not a little puppy but nothing over age two, and not a biter or a dog who wants to chase a cat. It doesn't have to be a specific breed, but a nice dog, and a people dog—not a dog who would rather hang out with another dog."

"It's often larger dogs, like Labs or shepherds or something along those lines," Ron comments. "It's great, because the bigger dogs at our rescue are harder to place—more than half of all pet dogs in the US weigh less than twenty-five pounds—and we feel so good about them going to a program like Elana's rather than running loose at the farm for six months or longer before somebody will finally take them. The fact that they really do veterans some good makes it even better."

The good they do is immeasurable, Elana says enthusiastically. For instance, she explains, "They're taught to interrupt a panic attack. If a veteran feels one coming on, he can just tap his chest once or twice, and the dog will rush over and press on his chest. It looks like the dog is just giving a hug, but it's a kind of compression therapy—kind of like the way some dogs feel calmer during a storm when they're wearing a snug-fitting Thundershirt. But it's a real, living, breathing best friend. The dog might give you kisses as it's pressing against you. You can be walking down the street, feeling overwhelmed, and lean against a building, and the dog takes care of you. After a while, the veteran does not even have to tap his chest. The dog recognizes the energy changing around the person when a panic attack is starting. The veteran becomes paralyzed with fear, and the dog knows what to do.

"Different things trigger different veterans," Elana says. "Someone might see a can rolling on the street, and that could trigger something that happened in a market. Others can't drive under an overpass—they picture people plotting to attack them.

"The dogs help with night terrors, too—memories that just keep replaying. I've had veterans who are afraid to go to sleep because they're afraid of the night terrors—they wake up screaming, covered in sweat, utterly terrified. But a service dog will come over and lick them and bring them out of it. The dog always sleeps in the room with the veteran, some of the smaller ones right on the bed.

"They also help with crowds. Many veterans don't like feeling crowded—it's a trigger for them—and a dog can be taught to stand right in front of them like a block, so crowds can't push them or give them a feeling of suffocation."

Marks, an army veteran who served in Iraq, explains what it

means for him to have Ava, a German shepherd we found wandering the streets, belonging to no one. The letters of her name stand for **A Veteran's Angel.**

"I was diagnosed with agoraphobia and have trouble leaving the house," Marks says. "I'll go through this whole process, pacing back and forth, but she'll jump on me and calm me down, distract me from that feeling of anxiety coming up.

"She also distracts me from *me*. Everything is not about me in that moment. Let's say I'm having a panic attack. Right then I can say, 'I still have this dog that comforts me.' I like to rub her ears. I can focus strictly on her and tune out everything else around me. Petting her ears calms me down. It keeps me present. If I lose my ability to be present, that's when the panic attack starts. In the end she makes me feel focused. I can even get in and out of stores really quick.

"She represents a new chapter in my life, and I'm learning how to have feelings for other people. I feel like there's a barrier between me and other people, but I'm starting to be able to feel. I'm not scared to branch out and try something new and go past my limitations.

"Probably the most beautiful thing about the whole process is that she makes me forget bad things. The dog was thrown away, and I felt thrown away. We each had limited communication, but somehow we have to make this work. Together we heal each other. It makes me less selfish because the dog relies on me as much as I rely on her."

We did not speak to other veterans who have a Danny & Ron dog that has become a service dog, because the aim of Elana's program is to help veterans live peaceably, not revisit things that could potentially bring up bad memories and keep them mired in trauma or create any unnecessary duress. We were grateful that Marks felt comfortable enough to open up.

A veteran's emotional comfort is so paramount to Elana that when he or she brings home a service dog, her organization gives him or her everything needed: leashes, dog food, dog bowls, toys, a dog bed. "No stress that way," she says.

But while we didn't speak with any more veterans directly about their experiences, some of the anonymous comments on her website provide further testimony. Veterans from all branches of the military talk about such things as finally being able to go out during the daytime again, about reconnecting emotionally with their children and doing things with them they hadn't been able to do, or going to see a fireworks display. One veteran said his dog had rescued him from despair and gave him new hope in life.

Elana helps veterans not only of recent conflicts such as those in Iraq and Afghanistan but also some from the Vietnam War. Veterans with PTSD are receiving more help than they once did, she says, but "not enough. Many times they're pushed to the back." We are proud to partner with her in her work, if only in a small way.

We are also pleased to be able to help Meals on Wheels of the Palm Beaches, which serves Florida's Palm Beach County. Many of the organization's clients are not able to afford food for their pets.

The organization's president and executive director, Pamela Calzadilla, explains, "The seniors we serve, with an average age of eighty-three and some over one hundred, were giving their own food to their dogs and cats. They were living on the edge, just above the poverty mean, and were going hungry to hold on to their animals."

It made sense that they would go to that length, Pamela says. "Seniors can be lonely, especially homebound seniors who live alone, which is basically who we serve, and surveys have found that having a pet in the home increases happiness, increases your life span, gives you purpose."

But pet food wasn't even the biggest challenge, Pamela reports. The biggest obstacle was veterinary care, ranging from teeth cleanings and annual shots to very expensive surgeries. "Our clients just couldn't afford the fees. The grants that Danny and Ron have given us—I can't tell you what a huge help it has been, letting clients keep their pets when they might not otherwise have been able to," she says.

Carolyn Searle can speak to the benefit directly. Eighty-one-years old, she lives with her Pomeranian/cocker spaniel mix Candy in a Royal Palm Beach apartment on $1,018 a month, $900 of which goes toward rent. "Out of the $118 I have left, I have to pay for my electric and phone and all my paper goods, so having to buy the dog food would really cost me a lot of money," she says.

Candy used to eat some of Carolyn's food, but now she has her own. "They send me a bag every month," she says.

"I love my dog," Carolyn relates. "I'd die without her. She sticks with me like glue. She sleeps with me every night, and during the day she's either on my chair with me or underneath the chair. When I cook she sits right by me in the kitchen. When I'm in the bathroom, she's right by my side. I can't walk that much—I use a cane and a walker—but I take her right outside and she does her business. I also have paper by the door in case I can't get up in time in the morning. I've had her since she was eight weeks old. I would never get rid of her." What Carolyn means is that she'd sooner resort to going without food herself than relinquish her pet.

Another client of the Meals on Wheels "Animeals" program that we support in Palm Beach is eighty-year-old Vietnam War veteran Michael Blumenau. He receives food for his silver-blue Maine coon cat called Blu, whom he has had since she was two days old. "She's on my chest right now," he says, talking with us.

When asked how he feels about his pet, he responds, "Let's put it this way: she's my companion, my little girlfriend. When I moved into the apartment from the house, she ran away. Two days later I went back to the house looking for her, and she jumped right into my arms. I had tears in my eyes from the time she ran off until I found her. I love this little cat. Every time I take a shower she's on the back of the tub on the platform. When I go in to watch television on the couch, she'll come right into the living room and get on my lap and sit there with me. She stays right by my side."

Michael explains that he has nerve pain in his left leg that makes it hard for him to walk. "I'm only a couple of blocks away from the supermarket," he says, "but it takes me two hours to get there and back. Meals on Wheels provides me with bags of cat food. It really helps."

Lately, he adds, "With my leg hurting, Blu will sleep between my knee and my foot to keep my foot warm. I've lost blood flow there. She is so good. I adore her. I wouldn't let anything happen to this cat."

Helping people keep their pets is extremely important to us. "If someone already has a dog or cat, we don't want them to be in a position to have to try to find a good home for their pet," Danny says. "The pet already has a good home. And more dogs and cats are saved by staying put because they will remain safest with the people who wanted them in the first place. They won't end up slipping through the cracks as a result of being dropped off at a shelter."

That's also why we started giving tens of thousands of pounds of pet food to food banks and to newly homeless people during the pandemic. We want folks to be able to keep their dogs with them.

Some other ways in which we have been able to step up to help since the movie debuted have played out closer to home. For instance, we learned through our rescue channels that a county shelter for dogs on the grounds of a prison within a day's drive was not being properly maintained. We were told the dogs had not been fed for a while, so we went there with our bus and our own local shelter. The dogs were wallowing in twelve to fourteen inches of feces and urine. The only way for them to avoid the piles and pee was to jump up into barrels swinging from a rope. "Danny and I almost threw up a couple of times, the smell was so bad," Ron says. "They were violating all kinds of animal-care ethics."

"Most of the dogs were so scared," Danny comments.

"We had to pry them out of the barrels to save them. They were swinging on the line," Ron notes.

We wound up rebuilding a lot of the kennels—new concrete and new fencing. We helped modernize the kennel runs, too. And fortunately, our presence ended up making for some long-term changes. Previously, we never came across a shelter director. The prisoners were just told to throw the dogs some food. It was all very unsanitary, very unsafe, with horrible conditions if it became really cold at night or really hot during the day. There were hardly any overhangs or other build-outs to protect the dogs from the weather. But they finally hired someone part-time to head the rescue operation and improved the infrastructure for the animals. Community embarrassment after the deplorable conditions were exposed brought desperately needed financial resources to the situation.

In another case, we needed to rescue a dog and her puppies from someone who wasn't taking proper care of them, and we had to set humane traps to try to catch them all. "It was a very sad area," Ron says. "All of these mobile homes, most of them with zero windows in them and no air-conditioning. Just people sitting outside."

"It was a little bit like a *Deliverance* feeling," Danny adds. "We felt like we were being watched out of the trailers with their boarded-up windows."

Making it all odder still was that as we were trying to get the dogs' owner to talk to us, to trust us, we noticed signs all over people's yards: "Marriage is between a man and a woman"; "God hates queers." Davis, the filmmaker, who is married to a man named Luis, happened to be with us, trying not to laugh as we negotiated. It was all pretty surreal—but we managed to retrieve the dogs and bring them home to take care of them.

We have also been able to help people farther afield. One couple we came across on Facebook.

"It all started with our son dying," recounts Phil Matzen of Central Islip, New York. "He was a little under four months old; his name was Philip Junior. We had a recalled bassinet, except we didn't know it. He rolled over and suffocated. Days later there was a storm, and our neighbor's fence went down. Our dog, a Rottweiler named T Rex, ran through the opening and out into the street and was severely injured in a hit-and-run.

"We didn't have a lot of savings, because we literally had just buried our son. That used up most of our money. I brought Rex to an animal hospital, and that ate every dollar we had left—two thousand. They took X-rays and did some other diagnostics and put him in a splint, but he still needed surgery or he was going to have to be put down. He couldn't walk. Having just lost our son, he was all we had left. He was still a puppy, just eighty pounds at that point, and I had to carry him outside to go to the bathroom because he couldn't walk after the accident.

"A friend made us a GoFundMe page, which I shared on Facebook. Danny & Ron's Rescue reached out to me. I'll be honest—at first I thought it was a scam. You see so many of them. By that point we had accumulated, like, $2,500, but the surgery was going to cost $8,000. They offered to pay for the whole thing."

"I kept saying, 'But you don't even know us. Why would you do this for us?'"

Phil's wife, Kiara, was just as incredulous. "Are you serious?" she asked. When we told her we were, she responded, "This is crazy. I can't believe this! I'm so overwhelmed. We are so grateful. There's nothing I can say to express our gratitude enough. I know somehow our angel is looking down on us and sent you to us. We would like to send you a thank-you card from our son's funeral with a personal note on the back."

That was three years ago. Now fully grown, Rex weighs between 120 and 130 pounds. "When I tell people he almost lost his leg they don't believe me," Phil says. "He has a scar going from the inside of his hip all the way down to the inside of his foot, and he has a metal rod in his leg. But you should see the way this dog swims and jumps."

Rex now lives with Gizmo, a little nine-pound Boston terrier who terrorizes him. He also lives with Phil and Kiara's daughter, Dylan, who was born a little more than a year after Phil Junior died. *All* the scars have been healing, and we are very glad to have been able to be a part of that.

We are also glad to report that as we have been broadening our own horizons, it seems the release of the film has helped others broaden theirs. Very soon after the movie hit Netflix, a viewer got in touch with us to say that she had always thought there was something wrong with gay people but now feels that she had been wrong. She wanted us to know she was going to look at things through a different prism, saying that what was important was kind behavior toward animals and a loving spirit. We are all the same, she said she now realized, just trying to live our best lives, and she wished us Godspeed as we went forward in our mission.

We've heard from others as well, some in person. One gentleman walked up to us upon recognizing us and told us that throughout his entire life with his son, he had always felt there was a disconnect; something kept them apart. After watching the movie, he thought, could his son possibly be gay and not want to tell him? He spoke to his other children about his concern and they told him, "My God, Dad, you didn't know he was gay?"

The man said he felt so much guilt—and so foolish for not realizing that possibility about his child. Worse still, he said, he felt ashamed that he had "presented a front" that made his son afraid to tell him.

He wound up talking to his son—a young adult by that point—letting him know he had seen the film and explaining that he felt bad that he hadn't been the kind of father his son could come to. Now, the man told us, he and his son have a great understanding between them and a closeness that had always been lacking.

So many people in the LGBTQ community have found themselves abandoned, or at least marginalized or misunderstood, by their families, by others. It's good to know that rescue—being loved, living with dignity, *belonging*—is happening on more than one front.

"I love this little cat. I wouldn't let anything happen to her," says Vietnam War veteran Michael Blumenau, who feeds his Maine coon, Blu, with financial assistance from Danny & Ron's Rescue.

Carolyn Searle used to feed her dog, Candy, some of her own food, but with a contribution to Meals on Wheels of the Palm Beaches by Danny & Ron's Rescue, Candy now has her own meals. "I'd die without her," Carolyn says.

"When Rex needed a surgery we couldn't afford, a friend made us a GoFundMe page, which I shared on Facebook," says Phil Matzen, pictured here with his wife, Kiara, their daughter, Dylan, and Rex. "Danny & Ron's Rescue reached out to me," Phil says. "I'll be honest—at first I thought it was a scam. You see so many of them. By that point we had accumulated, like, $2,500, but the surgery was going to cost $8,000 or Rex would have to be put down. They offered to pay for the whole thing."

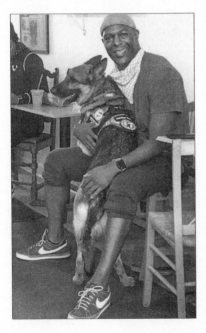

Army veteran Marks and his dog, Ava, who was saved by Danny & Ron's Rescue and then sent to the Chicago-based War Dogs Making It Home to be paired with a former soldier as a service dog. Says Marks of Ava: "She makes me forget bad things."

In Aruba with our friend Natalya Yermak, who runs New Life for Paws there much the way we run Danny & Ron's Rescue. Every year we take a couple of dogs from her for rehabilitation and adoption in the States. This year we brought back Breeze (in Ron's arms), who needed surgeries in both her hind legs, and Almond (held by Danny), who had to have an eye removed.

Chapter 14

Lifetime Promise

We're running behind this morning. Buttercup—the papil-lon mix Ron took home from the shelter when he saw her owner disdainfully relinquish her in 2001—was throwing up in the night. Now well into her twenty-first year and the oldest dog we have ever had, she is in kidney failure and suffers from bouts of nausea. Ron supplements her fluid intake with an IV drip a couple of times a day, but the disease is getting the better of her.

On top of that, we took in twenty-five more dogs just two days ago. They were being abused in a hoarding situation, and right now we're at one hundred fourteen dogs—way over capacity and the most we've ever had at any one time. We're scrambling to get them adjusted and comfortable.

We have equestrian clients already waiting for us at the farm but can talk with you while we drive over from the doghouse.

One thing we wanted to share is that Phyllis, the last of the six hundred Katrina dogs that Nora Thomas of Seattle took from us so many years ago, died recently at the age of twenty. Nora was heartbroken, as were we.

"It was crushing," she says. "It was really—it was the hardest thing other than watching your parents die. I was with her at the end. It's still hard to talk about," she says, choking up. Worse still, Nora tells us, "When Phyllie went, Bugsy stopped eating. He had had oral cancer for about a year, but her passing really did him in. I had to put him to sleep three days after Phyllis."

Nora's family dealt with their grief by choosing another dog a month or so later. Some people need more time, some less. It's all okay. The right amount of time for bringing home a next dog to love is the time anyone requires. There's no prescription, and everyone should go with their instincts.

"My family and I were looking at Danny and Ron's new posts on Facebook," Nora says, "and we came across a Chihuahua mix named Kaylee. So my son Harry and I got on a flight and flew to the doghouse in South Carolina—we had never actually been to the house itself—and took her back home. Maisy Daisy had her pinned at first. She thought Kaylee was a little toy. But now they're fine.

"As for the doghouse, the place is like a heaven for dogs. It's just amazing to go there and see all these animals. I felt like I was walking into a rehab for the emotionally troubled. The dogs all come up to you and want to tell you their stories."

If only everybody could be like Nora, treating dogs with the love and dignity they deserve, and offering them the security and tenderheartedness they're entitled to. But the truth is that more than 3 million companion dogs enter shelters each year, and fewer than half of those are adopted. Almost 700,000 healthy dogs are euthanized.

That's why it's so important to us that young people learn about the importance of spaying and neutering dogs. It's part of our strategic plan, in fact. A couple of years ago we hired a husband-and-wife team with expertise in guiding nonprofit organizations, Bob and Noel Stanek, and when they helped us lay out the things we want to accomplish that go beyond our own rescue of dogs, education of children landed high up on the list. We want the generation growing up now to enter adulthood as responsible animal lovers.

One of our aims is to start a junior board composed of teens so they can participate in outreach to other youths about the critical importance of spay/neuter programs. We also want to explore the possibility of introducing materials on spay/neuter to schools and various extracurricular programs for children. Imagine a world a generation or two from now that didn't require shelters or euthanasia of healthy animals because every single dog alive was *supposed* to be born and live in a household that couldn't wait to love it and treat it with kindness and compassion rather than become another statistic in an overpopulation epidemic.

The very hardest part of what we have to do is choose which dogs come home with us, because every single choice to take a dog and rehabilitate it is also a choice to leave another one behind. "There are so many hours and hours of heartbreaking, painful agony when we come upon dogs that have been so badly abused, so badly neglected, and we can't tend to all of them," Ron says. "Some are so unhealthy that they die before we are even able to get them medical help. In your mind you can justify the logical end about not having any more space, but the emotional end is very hard to swallow."

Danny adds, "We just wear guilt because we don't have enough time to do every dog we encounter the justice he deserves. Even the ones we take in we don't have enough time for, which is why we want to adopt them out."

"Making it harder still is that their capacity to love is unbelievable," Ron comments. "They come with so much baggage—from abuse and other situations in which they have been treated so badly that they have no reason to ever trust a human being. And yet they do. They can open themselves up and give unconditional love even with all they have been through. They have no voice, but anyone who takes a rescued dog *gives* it a voice, lets the dog know that they 'hear' and understand what it has been through."

That's the backdrop against the *Lifetime Promise* we made to ourselves and on behalf of the rescue many years ago: that a dog deserves to spend its entire life valued, never knowing either material want or emotional insecurity, and we do our best to make sure that's the case for every single dog that comes into our hands.

As part of our promise, we also want to promote compassionate treatment of dogs not only by advocating for adoption whenever possible by also by putting an end to puppy mills, neglect, abuse, and dog fighting. The indelible impression left on Ron as a young man when he lost his Jack Russell terrier Sunny to thieves who stole her as dog-fighting bait makes the abolishment of dog fighting a particular priority for us.

"They mean what they say about their promise," Bob Stanek says. "A promise is defined in two ways: as a pledge or commitment and also as a cause, or grounds for hope. Danny and Ron are the living embodiment of both. They avow that the dogs they rescue will never again live in a shelter, never be needy, and never not be loved. They are amazing people. They started this thing from nothing, mortgaged their home. It's hard for them to ever say no.

"They adopted out one dog to an eighty-years-plus World War Two Normandy vet living in a flat three stories up without an elevator. He called one day and said, 'Ron, I can't keep this dog.' 'What's the problem?' Ron asked. The man told him he just couldn't go up and down the stairs several times a day anymore to take the dog for walks. What did Danny and Ron do? They went and hired a dog walker for the rest of the man's life so the pet could stay with the person he had come to love, the person who had given him a good home."

"Their hearts are so big," Noel Stanek says. "They don't want to see *anyone* suffer or struggle."

The executive director of the rescue, Nukhet Hendricks (hired with Noel and Bob's help after going through hundreds of applications, seventeen of them from lawyers), sees it the same way. "They truly do believe in a lifetime promise, that a dog deserves the affection and care it gets in their home and beyond. They'll do anything for the dogs they save or otherwise reach out to. It's no different from what you see in the film—times ten.

"They know the name of every single dog in their care, even though there are usually a hundred dogs in the house at a time. They will cook homemade meals for the dogs if that's what it takes for them to get the proper nourishment. And, of course, when they help a dog that someone adopts, that adopter's heart is being mended. Everything is interdependent. Helping a person is a by-product of helping a dog.

"Danny and Ron are there for their staff, as well," Nukhet

says. "They will help out financially from their own pockets if someone needs assistance, even if there is not a dog involved. And to this day they won't accept a salary from the rescue. They have the horse business for their own livelihood."

We would never take money from the dogs, which is why a salary from the rescue is out of the question. But what we do is not enough, and it's not false modesty that makes us say that. "Our lives are really just a moment," Danny comments. "If we don't think about who will stand up for the dogs after we're gone, then everything we've tried to do will have been futile from the beginning."

Ron agrees. "We want protection and care of dogs to be a legacy that goes on, not just something that happened during the brief moment of our own lives."

That's why, while we've saved and adopted out close to 14,000 dogs over the years and hope to do the same for many more, it can't stop with us. It's the reason we want to reach out more to young people and also the reason part of our plan is preparing for the security of Danny & Ron dogs in the future. When Noel and Bob first joined our organization a few years ago, they asked us, "Where do you want to be in a year? In three years? In ten years? What do you want to happen to the rescue when you're gone?"

That helped us structure things so that if we were to die tomorrow, the rescue would continue to go on the way it always has. We've left the doghouse to Danny & Ron's Rescue and provided for it financially so that even when we're not here as its founders, it can keep operating. People stay at the house now when we're away at horse shows, including the three-month-long Winter Equestrian Festival. The place is never unattended, and that doesn't have to end.

We also hope to partner collaboratively with other groups involved in rescue, maybe even creating other Danny & Ron doghouses, not just in the United States but also in other countries. We believe that working together to further the mission of treating all dogs with love and respect would make for a stronger initiative and better results than different rescues trying to make a go of it on their own. That, too, would extend to the dogs what they deserve beyond our own moment on earth. It would take care of their future generations. Even rescues coming together to have workshops on the best way to save dogs and treat them well would strengthen the effort and help it to snowball well into the future.

Not that it seems in the plans for either of us to be going anywhere just yet. We've got too much to do. In fact, we've just reached the gate at the bottom of the driveway leading to Beaver River Farm and really have to get on with the day.

The farmhouse is now more than one hundred years old—a veritable antique. And the tender little live oak saplings that lined the drive when Danny first bought the place are today more than fifty feet tall, striking an almost balletic pose with limbs stretched gracefully upward as they form a magnificent canopy overhead. They are so tall and dense, in fact, that they hide the farmhouse from view until you get much closer. Still, we are able to see our clients waiting off to the side.

Yes, we're late, but they need to wait just a few more minutes. First, Danny will feed the chickens some leftover casserole from last night's dinner and will also give some snacks to the mules in the back fields, behind the barn. These days there's Edwina and Booker T, and both particularly like carrots.

Ron will make his way over to the side fields to give treats to the cows. We currently have Lucy and Ethel, a mother-daughter pair of miniature Herefords, red with white heads, who were about to be loaded into a slaughter truck in Pennsylvania. They both had very serious upper respiratory infections, so we sent them to one of the country's top clinics for large animals, where they recuperated for about six to seven weeks before we had them shipped to the farm. (Any animals we save that are not dogs we save with our own money. Danny & Ron's Rescue is strictly for dogs.)

We also have Mayhew, daughter of a dairy cow named Charlotte who supposedly couldn't get pregnant and therefore couldn't produce milk and was also going to be slaughtered. Skinny and run-down-looking, the gentle black-and-white heifer settled in one year while we were down in Wellington at the Winter Equestrian Festival. Then, one day in February, Ron received a call from someone who worked on the farm. "I have some bad news for you," he said.

"Your heart stops," as Ron describes it. "Your stomach turns. 'What happened?'" he asked. It turned out Charlotte had given birth. The farmhand thought we'd be upset about having another bovine mouth to feed. On the contrary, we were thrilled! Charlotte died only a year later, unfortunately, but Mayhew, the spitting image of her, lives on.

As does Zena. A South African miniature cow known as a zebu, she was found bloodied with her horns missing at the side of the road. Ron will feed her and her pasture mates apples cut into eighths. "'Come on, girls,' I'll say as I head over," Ron relates, "and they'll all start mooing and running over toward the railroad-tie fence."

Ron will also give treats to Jackson, a rescue from a Thoroughbred racetrack, and two horse show retirees, Regan and Alf, who had very successful careers. Usually the horses receive carrots, but sometimes mints are thrown in, too.

Dogs scamper down the driveway to greet us as we unlatch the front gate. Moonpie and Johnny Cake are long gone, of course, but others have taken their place many, many times over during the last forty-three years. Today gentle brown mutt Katana has come to be stroked on the muzzle, as has Randy the hound mix, Benji the Great Pyrenees/ Lab cross with the sad eyes, St. Bernard/ Irish setter beauty Hutch, and sweet Remi the blue heeler—each of them waiting to be taken into their forever home.

We're happy to oblige their request for a little attention before the day gets under way. They don't know it yet, but it's going to be an exciting morning for them. The farrier is coming, and they like to watch.

Danny feeds the mules. They like carrots.

Ron with Buttercup, the longest-lived dog our rescue has ever had.

The tender, little live oak saplings that lined the drive when Danny first bought the farm are now all grown up and more than fifty feet tall.

Epilogue

Cotton has already done his dance, gotten chased around the mattress (he would giggle at this game of tag if he could), received his treat in his crate, and climbed back up onto the bed to take his place on Danny's pillow, ready for Danny to wear him like a hat. Speckles assumes the position as Ron's hat, while Meer Meer and now Sweet Pea keep sentry nearby. As they see it, the top of the bed is "base." No one is allowed to bother them there.

Wiggling goes on as well, as some of the dogs cocoon themselves tightly under the covers. The little bumps and lumps under the sheet remind us exactly where we have been left a little space to wedge ourselves in.

Isabelle hasn't entered the bedroom yet, but she will. She

wants the space quiet first, and she also doesn't appreciate any moving about as she gets settled. She still positions herself at the far corner; it will be her decision about whether she ever wants to nestle closer.

Beanie—she's still having a tough go of it. She has already poked her head into the room twice but then retreated. It's hard to watch her too scared to indulge in something that intrigues her, but we sense that it won't be long before she takes a great leap of faith.

It is already past eleven, and we *have* to get some sleep. Tomorrow is going to be especially busy. Jelly Bean, a soulful thirty-pound mixed breed who chooses to sleep in the living room, is going to see a veterinary cardiologist about his heart murmur. He may need a higher dose of medicine. And little Yorkshire terrier mix Lionel has had another seizure. Is he on the right drug? Should we take him to the neurologist for a recheck?

We also have a family coming to look at Meryl, a cream-colored corgi mix. Her adoption has to be in person because she's an extremely energetic dog, and we don't want her to go off somewhere and then have to be concerned. What some adopters say doesn't matter does, they later realize, and it is sometimes better to have a potential adopter see a dog in action before making a decision.

We crawl into bed more than ready for some shut-eye, willing to let the concerns go for a few hours. Normally we fall right to sleep, but something feels . . . not quite right. What is it? We look at each other but realize we have to let it go. Whatever it is, it'll come to us.

And then, *bam*, Busy Bee flings herself onto the bed as if finishing up some kind of complicated high-wire act and plopping to the net. Snuggling right between us, she falls fast asleep as Danny rubs her belly and Ron strokes her ears. We were right. It *has* been a good day.

Forever Home <3.

Join Us in the Lifetime Promise

This book may have come to an end, but the story of dogs needing tender care and loving homes has not. Join us in the Lifetime Promise. Find us at our website, dannyronsrescue.org, or on Facebook, Instagram, or Twitter (@dannyronsrescue).

Acknowledgments

Danny & Ron and Larry Lindner thank: Our savvy and forward-thinking agent Susan Canavan of the Waxman Agency, who knew before we did that there was a book in this story when she and her family happened to see *Life in the Doghouse* on a Jet Blue flight from the Virgin Islands back to Boston; and our deft editor Sydney Rogers of HarperOne, who was on board with the vision from the get-go and with a gentle but skillful touch guided us in nudging the right words into just the right places.

We also want to acknowledge here our superb copy editor, John McGhee, and HarperOne art director Adrian Morgan and the team at The Book Designers, who nailed the cover by making terrific use of Julie Prickett's exquisite photography. Their work immediately made us want to hold the book in our hands.

Danny & Ron thank: The many thousands of adopters of Danny & Ron dogs both in the United States and around the world. We are more grateful than we could express that you have given them a home of their own, a family, and a place where they can feel safe and secure and loved for the rest of their days. We also thank the donors throughout the US and from forty-eight countries on five continents; your contributions support our work in countless ways. And we thank those who spread the word about Danny & Ron's Rescue—a very valuable contribution in itself.

Acknowledgments

Our entire equestrian community gets kudos and love many times over for always being at our side and for pitching in every inch of the way—with adoptions, contributions, and publicity—as far back as the Katrina days. You have greatly helped make the rescue the success it has been. Special thanks here to all the horse show managements that welcome our rescue dogs to their events in order to help them find their forever homes.

With much appreciation we mention Karen Odom, our very first staff member, who stands with us in our efforts to this day; and Michael Schofield, for all his years of dedication in service to the dogs—and for keeping the highways hot! We simply could not do what we do without you and the rest of the Danny & Ron team here at home.

Likewise, we heartily thank the staff at Beaver River Farm, who thought they were coming there solely to take care of horses but willingly took on the dogs—with aplomb and good cheer.

Brenda Miller, "ruler of the fort" who has done our books for more years than we can count, how could we ever express our appreciation for the endless hours you have provided to keep us glued together? Ditto to Bobbi Bagley, whose acuity with numbers has taken us through internal audits, monthly budgeting, and all the other high-wire finance details that come with running a rescue.

Sharon Jones, who served as director of Camden's Kershaw County Animal Shelter for almost as many years as we have been Danny and Ron, thank you for your truly boundless love of animals—and for your friendship. In the same breath we bow our heads in memory of Judy Thiel, who would regularly write checks to keep the shelter afloat after she donated the funds to build it once the old, disease-ridden facility had finally been shut down.

Acknowledgments

Danny & Ron marketing director Kim Tudor, for your vision that helped us grow, for your determined spirit that allowed us to climb metaphorical mountains, and for your uncanny ability to match the right dogs with the right homes and keep the traffic moving, we can only say that words of thanks are inadequate.

Danny's niece, Christy Edens, your superpowers for saving dogs and your heart of gold—which you share with the rescue every single day and with us personally—keep everyone going through even the very hardest of times.

Board member Danielle McCluskey, without you we'd still be Danny and Ron—a couple that rescues dogs, not Danny & Ron's Rescue, a bona fide nonprofit organization. The day you reached out was a day that changed our lives—and, more importantly, the lives of thousands and thousands of dogs.

The rest of our board has also helped out in ways too numerous to count. For your devotion to the animals, thank you (in alphabetical order) Ramon Arani, Stacey Arani, Penelope Ayers, Janice Cannizzo, Lannie Lipson, and Caroline Moran.

Of course, many thanks go as well to our patient and hardworking executive director Nukhet Hendricks, who daily keeps Danny & Ron's Rescue on course. We're so thankful for your literally endless hours of dedication. And Noel and Bob Stanek, where would we be without your knowledge, wisdom, and guidance?

Elena Portu and your daughters, Sophia and Ana, much gratitude for spending time with so many of the rescue dogs and for being readily available to child-test them before we recommend them to families with young children.

Anne Caroline Valtin, thank you for your years of friendship and dedication to our rescue mission.

Acknowledgments

Judy Arnold Resner, we are so appreciative of all your expertise. And Brenda and Jim Scamordella at Paws for Seniors, we owe you so much for taking so many older dogs from us—and for rescuing us that time our bus broke down on the way to Virginia! Jennifer Chopping, you are so wonderful for all the canine lives you help save. And John Martino, your professional expertise and hands-on training of dogs we have needed help with—all for free—has made that many more dogs adoptable.

And now for the veterinarians. Dr. Ronnie Fulmer and veterinary assistant Rebecca Fulmer, how could we ever adequately express our appreciation for the endless hours you have put into saving our animals, for taking care of dogs with parvo, even for staying overnight with the dogs to make sure they were okay? Who *does* that? Dr. Matt Jenerette and the entire staff at the Camden Veterinary Hospital, your love and devotion for all of our dogs and your ability to save them and maintain their health heals us as much as it heals the animals. The entire staff of CVETS in Columbia, South Carolina, you have pulled so many dogs back from the brink. And Dr. Margaret Biggs, you are tops for taking care of all the dogs we bring to Florida for the Winter Equestrian Festival—and all the dogs we come across and end up bringing back to South Carolina.

Speaking of the Winter Equestrian Festival also means speaking of CeCe Levy, who runs the adoption booth for us there every year. And it means a shout-out to Susan Weisman, not only an all-hands-on-deck person at the booth but also a true saver of the underdogs. When we are overloaded, she will foster dogs that need extra attention.

Winters in Wellington also mean time spent with outgoing board member Jennifer Smith, who with current board member

Caroline Moran organizes the annual Martinis & Mutts fundraiser for Danny & Ron's Rescue. Thank you, both!

And thank you Kim Kolloff, for your beautiful vision about teaching kids the rewards of giving back through Lip Sync—and for the closeness we get to share with you.

Dr. Betsee Parker, our gratitude to you as the first person ever to turn your horse winnings over to the dogs—you have always been such a wonderful patron of the cause.

So many companies have stepped up, too. Jake's Pet Supply, run by Harry and Stacey Gelkopf in Lake Worth, sells us everything *at cost*—collars, dog beds, crates, toys. . . . They keep the shipments coming and don't make a dime on us! Jane De-Meulemester of Bannixx Pet Care Products donates thousands and thousands of dollars in shampoos and medicines for ear infections, hot spots, and other health issues all year long. R & L Carriers (thanks to the family of Roby Roberts) sends us pallet after pallet of free supplies—not just for dogs but also for cats, fish, and other animals. Essex Classics, which makes shirts for equestrians, designs a new line of shirts every year with our logo and a dog motif, and then makes a donation to Danny & Ron's Rescue for every single one sold—thank you Cathy Sacher!

Shapley Canine Care, with the wonderful administrative help of Sally Smith Burdett, donates dog care products, in addition to making cash donations. 1-800-Pet Meds offers financial support as well, in part by helping us open our adoption booth at the Winter Equestrian Festival. Marshall & Sterling Insurance, through our terrific contact Don Graves, helps via corporate sponsorship. Arnaud Henrard of machine manufacturer Foltex is yet another sponsor without whom we could not do the work we do.

Debi Fitzgerald, the beautiful new painting you produce for

our calendar cover each year keeps us in people's kitchens and workplaces throughout the land. For your arresting art that serves as a constant reminder of dogs in need, we can't thank you enough.

Natalya Yermak, kindred spirit, you thank us for the help we provide you, but we thank *you* for mirroring our work in Aruba at New Life for Paws—and for your friendship. Elana Morgan, our thanks go to you for your dedication to pairing service dogs with veterans at War Dogs Making It Home. You have given so many veterans—and dogs—a new and better life.

Gloria Gaynor, we could never repay you for your friendship, your love, and your dedication—both up front and behind the scenes. Nor, Stephanie Gold, could we ever make it up to you, not only for your friendship but also for all you have done to pull rabbits out of hats when doing so seemed impossible.

Filmmaker Ron Davis, for choosing to tap us on the shoulder and using your enormous talent to make *Life in the Doghouse* and put us on the map in a way we never could have imagined, *wow*! To the bottom of our souls, we will always be grateful. The warm friendship we developed with you in the process was a wonderful, unexpected bonus. Director and cinematographer Clay Westervelt, we are equally grateful for *your* talent and friendship.

Sal Scamardo and everybody else at FilmRise, you were just terrific at publicizing the dogs' cause and getting us in front of the camera everywhere from the *Today* show to the Hallmark Channel.

Finally, there's our coauthor, Larry Lindner. With humor and good will (and periodic shipments of cookies and carrot cake), Larry drew from us the bits and pieces of our lives and then turned them into storytelling that we couldn't be happier with.

We finally got to meet him in person when the pandemic had let up a bit and he was able to fly down to the doghouse. Most people walk in and immediately feel overwhelmed, but Larry got right to work falling in love with Jelly Bean, Beanie, Cotton, and the others—and they with him. The book was still in progress and there was a ways to go, but we knew then that we had chosen right—and managed to pick up a new friend along the way.

Larry Lindner thanks: Danny and Ron. What I love most about them is that they never sought acclaim for their efforts in rescue. Their tireless work on behalf of dogs and other animals comes from a place deep within; they'd be doing what they are doing whether or not anyone ever heard of them. I am honored that they let me into their lives, including the dark spaces, and honored more still to be considered one of their friends.

I thank, too, my son, John—the greatest "pup" ever to warm my home, and whose tenacious lobbying effort starting when he was hardly more than a tot is the reason we have more than one dog today. A like-minded soul, that one.

Finally, I thank my wife, Constance. There simply is no Larry without Constance—nor would there be dogs I've never met showing up in my kitchen from time to time. (And as long as we're being completely transparent, yes, it was Constance who backed up traffic near the town square that day to rescue a wounded squirrel.) Why I was lucky enough for her to enter my life that warm December afternoon on Lexington between 68th and 69th, I'll never know; I just happily tip my hat to fate.

About the Authors

Ron Danta and Danny Robertshaw, cofounders of Danny & Ron's Rescue, speak for animals who have no voice, having rescued and rehabilitated—right in their own home—some fourteen thousand dogs that came from shelters, puppy mills, dog-fighting rings, junkyards, and animal hoarders. They have also saved dogs chained to trees, near death at the side of the road, and separated from their human families during climate disasters. Danta and Robertshaw were designated ASPCA honorees of the year for their work in dog rescue and were also the corecipients of the *Robb Report* award for their animal rescue efforts. Subjects of the award-winning documentary *Life in the Doghouse*, they are now recognized internationally for their efforts to save dogs from cruel fates.

Danta has also earned acclaim for training equines and riders for championships at the Pennsylvania National Horse Show, Washington International Horse Show, Madison Square Garden, Devon, and other shows throughout the country. A horse trainer at the very top of his field, he is a three-time winner of the President's Distinguished Service Award from the United States Hunter Jumper Association. He was also named the US Hunter Jumper Association Volunteer of the Year. Additionally, he was recognized as *The Chronicle of the Horse* Show Hunter

Horseman of the Year and has been the subject of feature articles in numerous equine magazines.

Robertshaw made equestrian history when he was the first to win Champion in the Regular Working Hunter at Devon, Pennsylvania National, Washington International, Madison Square Garden, and the Royal Winter Fair all in the same year. He continued his winnings and subsequently received *The Chronicle of the Horse* Horseman of the Year award and was also the winner of the United States Equine Federation's Emerson Burr Trophy as well as the Daniel P. Lenehan Trophy for Judging. Additionally, Robertshaw received the US Hunter Jumper Association's Lifetime Achievement award. He has been inducted into the National Show Hunter Hall of Fame and The Carolina Hall of Fame and has been covered extensively in major equestrian magazines.

Larry Lindner is a *New York Times* bestselling collaborative author. He also penned a long-running, widely syndicated column for *The Washington Post* and a column for *The Boston Globe*. His writing has appeared in *Condé Nast Traveler;* the *Los Angeles Times; Reader's Digest; O, the Oprah Magazine;* and many other publications.